The Women's Movement in Community Politics in the U.S.

Pergamon Titles of Related Interest

Baehr   WOMEN AND MEDIA
Bauer & Ritt   FREE AND ENOBLED
Shaffer   WOMEN IN THE TWO GERMANIES

Related Journals *

WOMEN'S STUDIES INTERNATIONAL QUARTERLY
INTERNATIONAL JOURNAL OF INTERCULTURAL RELATIONS

*Free specimen copies available upon request.

PERGAMON
POLICY
STUDIES

ON SOCIAL ISSUES

The Women's Movement in Community Politics in the U.S.
The Role of Local Commissions on the Status of Women

Debra W. Stewart

Published in cooperation with the
Center for the American Woman and Politics,
of The Eagleton Institute of Politics,
Rutgers University

Pergamon Press
NEW YORK • OXFORD • TORONTO • SYDNEY • PARIS • FRANKFURT

Pergamon Press Offices:

U.S.A.	Pergamon Press Inc., Maxwell House, Fairview Park, Elmsford, New York 10523, U.S.A.
U.K.	Pergamon Press Ltd., Headington Hill Hall, Oxford OX3 0BW, England
CANADA	Pergamon of Canada, Ltd., Suite 104, 150 Consumers Road, Willowdale, Ontario M2J 1P9, Canada
AUSTRALIA	Pergamon Press (Aust.) Pty. Ltd., P.O. Box 544, Potts Point, NSW 2011, Australia
FRANCE	Pergamon Press SARL, 24 rue des Ecoles, 75240 Paris, Cedex 05, France
FEDERAL REPUBLIC OF GERMANY	Pergamon Press GmbH, Hammerweg 6, Postfach 1305, 6242 Kronberg/Taunus, Federal Republic of Germany

This research was supported by a grant from the Center for the American Woman and Politics, of The Eagleton Institute, Rutgers University. The grant was awarded in June 1976 and the field work was conducted during 1977.

Library of Congress Cataloging in Publication Data

Stewart, Debra W   1943-
   The women's movement in community politics in the U.S.

   (Pergamon policy studies)
   Bibliography: p.
   Includes index.
   1. United States.   President's Commission on the Status of Women. I. Title.
HQ1420.S78 1979   305.4'2'0973   80-14422
ISBN 0-08-025971-5

Printed in the United States of America

To my daughter,

Cynthia Vuille Stewart

Contents

Foreword

Debra Stewart's valuable study of local commissions on the status of women has roots in a social movement which, in effect, created her subject matter and also the mechanism by which she undertook research about it.

The women's rights movement of the late 1960s and 1970s focused on issues and made demands that resulted in the establishment of new commissions mandated to advise government about the needs and concerns of women in the community. While many women welcomed this development, the very existence of women's commissions stirred controversy in some quarters, raising ideological questions about appropriate strategies for promoting effective social reform, and political considerations about the relationship between government and pressure groups. Feminists and anti-feminists, liberals and conservatives, public officials and private citizens - from all directions, challenges emerged regarding the value and propriety of governmental commissions on women's status. Debate continues in the 1980s.

Professor Stewart's study deals with basic questions that should interest those concerned with the debate as it is related to the women's rights movement, to the institutionalization of women's issues within government, and to making judgments about the actual activities of women's commissions. What are the goals and agendas of local commissions on women's status? Who serves on them, and whose interests do they represent? How are they structured and supported? What have some of the commissions accomplished? Most important, Stewart brings a scholar's tools and perspective to bear on the issue of success: What accounts for it? How, why, and for whom have some commissions worked well?

The impact of the contemporary feminist movement has also been significant in the academic world. Research interests and activities aimed at developing new knowledge about women have grown rapidly over a little more than a decade. In 1973, the Center for the American Woman and Politics (CAWP) of the Eagleton Institute of Politics at Rutgers University announced a grants program to stimulate research and writing focused on women's participation in public life and government. The Florence Eagleton Grants Program came into existence at a time when few people could find support for conducting work about this subject. Indeed, some academicians did not consider it a serious area for legitimate scholarly inquiry.

The grants program was devised to provide financial and institutional resources to people capable of contributing knowledge to what CAWP did consider the important but neglected subject of women and politics. The topic announced by the grants program in 1976-77 was "Women and Local Government." Through its other educational, research, and public service programs, CAWP had become convinced that increasing numbers of women were discovering new opportunities for political participation and influence at local levels in communities everywhere. Yet the little visibility political women were receiving concentrated on what were perceived as the more glamorous, higher-level political arenas. By inviting proposals about women and local government, CAWP sought to call attention to women's public activities in entry level, grassroots positions across the country.

Debra Stewart's application to undertake a comparative analysis of local commissions on the status of women in several communities was one among approximately 200 interesting project proposals CAWP received from women and men across the country. It was selected as one of five projects awarded grants for a year's research. The original study supported by the Florence Eagleton Grant serves as the foundation for this book, but its contents extend beyond that study into an historical review and broad analysis of feminism and community politics as they encounter one another within the framework of women's commissions. Professor Stewart has now committed a great deal of energy over several years to the subject of governmental commissions on women's status. The Center for the American Woman and Politics is pleased to have played a role in assisting her to undertake this work.

Ruth R. Mandel
Director
Center for the American Woman and Politics

The Women's
Movement in
Community Politics
in the U.S.

1 Institutionalizing Female Participation: An Introduction

The women's movement taking shape in the last quarter of the twentieth century aims for equality, justice, and a more humane society. Few would dispute these worthy objectives, but noble ends alone seldom fund success. Ultimately success for the contemporary women's movement will turn on the capacity of feminists to mold political institutions toward movement ends.

Institutions are varied and access points are many on the American political scene. Today feminists of all shades are tugging at the levers of the system, hopeful of advancing in some incremental way the broad objectives of equality, justice, and humaneness. Through political action committees women are targeting candidates for election or defeat on the basis of their pro- or antifeminist stance. On other fronts women are acting through organized interest groups, bringing pressure to bear on government at all levels. Increasingly women are competing for office in all branches and levels of government, sometimes with considerable success. An ever-sharpening scholarly analysis gradually expands our understanding of the processes feminist activists employ and the impact they have achieved.

In two important spheres the contribution of committed feminist scholarship is substantial. In the area of movement politics, recent work deepens our insights into the necessary structural foundation for advancing feminist objectives.(1) Similarly in the analysis of female political roles a growing literature strongly advances understanding of how political women emerge and behave.(2) The unit of analysis in the first instance is "movement." In the second instance it is "women." Political institutions themselves and specifically institutions designed to enhance distaff interest and power have largely escaped scholarly feminist scrutiny. Yet since

1

knowing how to "work" the institutions of the system may produce ultimate success of movement objectives, this neglected plot in the increasingly well-plowed field of women in politics calls for committed laborers.

This study of local Commissions on the Status of Women was conceived with such a clear need in mind. (In recent years several commissions have dropped the term "Status" from their title. They designate themselves as a "Commissions for Women" or "Commissions on Women." In this essay "Commission on the Status of Women," the original and still widely used designation, is employed to characterize all official governmental commissions of this type.) Commissions on the Status of Women represent the sole governmentally endorsed effort to institutionalize systematically female participation in the United States. This work sets out to analyze critically that effort both by describing these institutions as part of the women's movement and by assessing their potential for serving as institutional levers for change.

The strengths and weaknesses of advisory commissions in general have some obvious bearing on the capacity of these particular commissions to advance women's movement ends. The citizen advisory board is a panel composed of private citizens and often government officials appointed to advise executives and legislative bodies at the local, state, and federal levels. Typically their mission is to focus attention on a pressing problem of some kind and to initiate new departures in problem solution.

The normative rationale for the advisory commission joins two values of participation and of representation. In a democracy participation is the process whereby citizens influence or control decisions affecting them.(3) More specifically it refers to "acts by those not formally empowered to make decisions . . . the acts being intended to influence the behavior of those who have such decisional power."(4) Representation in a democracy implies some form of standing in place of others, either descriptively, where the representatives constitute a mirror image of their constituencies, or substantively, where representatives stand for the interest of their constituents.(5)

Within the framework of these participation and representation concepts, commissions, as institutions, fulfill two distinct yet related functions. They provide a vehicle through which people can participate in influencing the outcome of public policy decisions, they create a kind of descriptive and interest representation inside government for specified groups.

Yet in recent years the value of advisory commissions for either their participatory or representational effect has been called into question. Critics argue that today the advisory commission has become "primarily a mechanism for broader elite participation in policy making and only indirectly a channel

through which the 'public,' in a broad sense participates."(6)
David Truman observes that notwithstanding the noble in-
tention that "individuals and groups likely to be affected
should be consulted before governmental action is taken,"(7)
the commission may in fact simply formalize access and restrict
the scope of conflict. In the popular press federal-level
commissions are often criticized as strongholds of special
interests or as vehicles for rewarding party loyalty.(8)
Perhaps the most damaging criticism of commissions is that
they live in constant danger of being coopted by their
sponsors - and that many succumb.(9) This cooptation
phenomenon has been strongly evident at the local level. In a
recent interview one 1960s civil rights activist in the South
reflected back on the uses of advisory commissions in small
southern towns during the early days of the civil rights
movement. "We would go into a town, begin to organize
people, and before you knew it the Mayor slapped up a 'Human
Relations Commission.'"(10) The obvious purpose of the
commission was to deflect pressure, suppress issues, and
generally promote the narrow political interests of appointing
officials.
       Thus the overall assessment of commissions as institutions
is mixed. On the one hand they promise to promote the values
of participation and representation in government. On the
other hand, the role they actually play in the political system
falls short of this ideal. But while debate about the effectiveness of the commission form goes on, governments throughout
the world proceed to adopt it as the principal mechanism for
magnifying the female voice in society. An overview of the
use of Commissions on the Status of Women beyond the borders
of the United States gives evidence of a broadly shared
commitment to this mechanism for expanding participation and
representation.

COMMISSIONS ON THE STATUS OF WOMEN:
HISTORICAL PERSPECTIVE

At the macro level the United Nations Commission on the Status
of Women symbolizes the international commitment to the
commission concept. Created in 1946, the UN commission is
mandated to promote women's political, economic, civil, social,
and educational rights and to make recommendations on "urgent
problems requiring immediate attention in the field of women's
rights, with the object of implementing the principle that men
and women shall have equal rights."(11) As originally
conceived the primary role of the UN commission was informa-
tional. But in addition to documenting the status of women in
member nations the commission coordinates efforts to secure

ratification of various UN and International Labor Organization (ILO) conventions on the treatment of women. Since the early 1960s it has also worked to promote the establishment of Commissions on the Status of Women at the regional and national levels.

Regionally the commission movement has met with only limited success. The earliest regional commission dates back to 1928 when the Inter-American Commission of Women was established under the Organization of American States. The Inter-American Commission has gained prominence for its considerable effort in reporting on problems limiting the contribution of women to the economic and sexual development of member countries. A more limited and apparently less successful regional endeavor was the Arab Women's Commission founded in 1971 under the auspices of the League of Arab States. Though regional commissions have been proposed in other parts of the world, efforts generally founder on the weaknesses of regions as units for launching stable programs.

At the national level, Commissions on the Status of Women have flourished, urged on by strong UN commission support. As early as 1963 the national commission gained international prominence when the UN Economic and Social Council passed a resolution calling the attention of member states to the "value of appointing national commissions on the status of women composed of leading men and women with experience in government service, education, employment, community development and other aspects of public life to develop plans and recommendations for improving the position of women in their respective countries." Consistently since 1963 the UN Economic and Social Council has called attention to national commissions as a vehicle for promoting the advancement of women worldwide.(12) By 1979, 35 countries reported some form of national commission and 32 additional countries indicated the establishment of women's divisions charged with commission-type functions, within the national administration.

In discussing national commissions, it is important to note that the commission form is not exclusively Western. Strong commissions exist in Africa, Asia, and the Middle East, as well as in Europe and throughout the western hemisphere. Of course the commission mandates vary in scope. For example, the Italian "National Consultative Commission on Problems of Women Workers" concerns itself principally with difficulties emerging as women increase their numbers in the labor force. In Britain, by contrast, the "Women's National Commission" enjoys a broad charge: "To ensure by all possible means that the informed opinion of women is given its weight in the deliberations of government and in public debate of matters of public interest, including in particular those which may be considered of special interest to women." The main disagreement that has developed among proponents of commissions

internationally is between those urging lay commissions that represent a cross section of informed opinion and those wanting well-staffed permanent women's bureaus.(13)   Nine countries have resolved this debate by maintaining both.
At this point in time no one can say definitively how commissions have shaped the course of change in the life experience of women across nations.   Clearly, however, the ultimate impact of commissions depends largely on their capacity to reach down into the life and culture of a society: to ask the right questions and to engage the right people in the change process.   In the United States, proponents of commissions have made a concerted effort to devolve the commission to a level closer to the society's grass roots.   State and especially local Commissions on the Status of Women express this effort and deserve close attention for what they may signal to the commission movement internationally.   The history of Commissions on the Status of Women in the United States recount the ubiquitous blending of pluses and minuses characteristic of the commission approach to bringing change more generally.

The American Experience

The Presidential Commission on the Status of Women was established by executive order of John Kennedy and signed on December 4, 1961.   The commission's announced purpose was "to examine and recommend remedies to combat the...prejudices and outmoded customs [that] act as barriers to the full realization of women's basic rights."(14)   The idea of appointing such a commission at this time seems to have been promoted by Esther Peterson, who, as assistant Secretary of Labor, was the highest ranking woman in the Kennedy administration.   The compelling rationale for launching this effort in 1961 was, however, political.
First, there were substantial numbers of women who had worked for Kennedy in 1960, none of whom received high administration appointments.   These women had to be given something in exchange for their efforts.   Second, it would be desirable to create a strong bloc of women who would campaign for Kennedy in 1964, and a commission of this kind could mobilize large numbers of women.   Third, some vehicle had to be found to get the Kennedy administration "off the hook" on the Equal Rights Amendment (ERA) issue.(15)
One staff member of the presidential commission reports this third element to be the principal catalyst.   Reflecting on his experience with the group, he charges: "They really didn't want equal rights for women....   The major purpose of the Presidential Commission on the Status of Women was to deflect the impetus for the ERA."(16)   Undeniably, President Kennedy

was deeply in debt to labor for his election in 1960, and labor at that time was strongly opposed to the ERA. The executive director of the commission, Esther Peterson, had close ties with labor, had served on the Kennedy campaign staff, and was the ideal choice to orchestrate the finessing of the ERA issue, if that was the administration's objective. Also lending credence to this jaundiced view is the fact that Emanuel Celler (D-NY) had first proposed the idea of a commission to study the status of women in the United States in 1946 and again in 1961, for the express purpose of generating data to support "killing the Amendment once and for all."(17)

Whatever the intended purpose of this first Commission on the Status of Women, the product of its 22-month study did not simply reinforce the status quo. Admittedly the commission report did take the position that the ERA was unnecessary, women's equality being already guaranteed by the fifth and fourteenth amendments. But analysts of the feminist movement rightly stress the schizophrenic character of the report overall:

> The most fundamental [assumptions of the report] presupposed that the nuclear family unit was vital to the stability of American society and that women have a unique and immutable role in that family unit; accordingly, women who work, and who are also married and possibly mothers, play a dual role in society to a much greater degree than do men who work and are also married and fathers. [Yet] another fundamental assumption of the Report was that, notwithstanding women's dual role, every obstacle to their full participation in society must be removed.(18)

While this latter assumption seems commonplace today, it drew heavy fire from "experts" on women at the time. In reviewing the commission report for the New York Times, Edward Eddy, president of Chatham College charged:

> The preoccupation with lifelong equality for the female...has led the commission down an unfortunate one-way street. It is both surprising and maybe even shocking to find a presidentially appointed group so completely misunderstanding the basic nature of its subject and so willing to capitulate to the demands of a materialistic society. Not a word is said about the power of women to shape ideas, to force the making of sound decisions, to act as the conscience of the world.... The Commission's startling denial of the right of women to be female is nowhere better illustrated than in the section on

education.... Evidently the need for a liberal
education is not considered important.(19)

On balance the impact of the presidential report can be
considered positive, in that at least it called attention to the
unfavorable condition of women in American society. Since the
facts, in large part, spoke for themselves, the final compilation of data presented in the report fulfilled many hopes of
the more change-oriented commission members. The activities
of the commission also generated institutional spin-offs. The
Citizens Advisory Council, established in accord with one of
the report recommendations, would in later years take the
staunch women's rights line that the presidential commission
was unable to take. More relevant from the perspective of
this study, the report spurred the Women's Bureau of the
United States Department of Labor to spearhead the establishment of state Commissions on the Status of Women.
    Working primarily through the heads of the Business and
Professional Women's Associations at the state level, the
Women's Bureau arranged for the matter of the status of
women to be brought to the attention of the governor in many
states, and, by 1966, 45 states had commissions studying the
condition of women within their jurisdictions. While the
number of "activists" on the presidential commission had been
limited, perhaps because the stakes for the appointing officials
were too high to risk such nominations, feminists found ample
representation on state commissions. In the absence of a
specific threat such as the ERA posed to the presidential
commission, governors manifested more concern with partisan
commitment than with political ideology.
    As a result, by the time of the third annual meeting of
the Commissions on the Status of Women in June of 1966, many
of the state commissioners attending were committed feminists.
This meeting was called under the auspices of the Citizens
Advisory Council and the Interdepartmental Committee on the
Status of Women, and members of this coordinating officialdom
warned strongly against the state commissions passing resolu-
tions contradicting official government positions. Disillusioned
as a consequence of working through governmental bodies, a
group of state commission members agreed to form a more
independent lobbying organization. Thus, the National
Organization for Women was born. The National Association of
Commissions on the Status of Women continues to function
today but only as a very loose umbrella organization. Primarily, it publishes a newsletter for the exchange of information
and coordinates a yearly conference of state and local
Commissions on the Status of Women.
    One scholar has aptly summed up the contribution of the
federal and state commissions in the 1960s by asserting that
they never "mustered the clout to shake up executive agencies

or to pressure Congress."(20)   Nonetheless, they did provide
a basic organizing framework which served to facilitate the
full-blown emergence of the women's movement in the late
1960s. Unlike their predecessors at the state and federal
levels, local Commissions on the Status of Women (CSWs),
proliferating in the early 1970s, developed in the context of a
heightened awareness produced by this women's movement.
      The first local Commission on the Status of Women in the
United States was formed in Beaver Dam, Wisconsin, in 1966.
By 1973, the Women's Bureau recorded 31 local commissions
across the country; three years later 82 were reported as
officially established. Most local commissions are in cities or
highly urbanized counties where various governmental units
have been consolidated.(21)   Chapter 2 will explore the
composition of these commissions and present profiles highlighting variation from locale to locale. But before turning to
this overview of local Commissions on the Status of Women some
justification for the exclusive focus on these local institutions
is in order.

LOCAL COMMISSION FOCUS: THE RATIONALE

The local sphere of government has always been perceived as
that part of the political system most accessible to women. A
significant factor in affording this accessibility is that local involvement is thought to require less "role dispensability" than
service at other levels in the political system. As a woman
moves from the federal, to the state, to the local scene,
official political involvement becomes increasingly compatible
with conventional female role behavior. While women active in
any public role doubtless experience some role strain, political
activism in the local community may still mesh with largely
unchanged family schedules and expectations. Moreover
women have conventionally expressed stronger interest in local
issues than in those of the more removed state and federal
arenas.(22) Women's interest in education is always cited to
buttress this point. Especially today local governmental
institutions are increasingly the first-level articulators and
interpreters of public policy vital to the life chances of
women and the scope of issues covered is broad, ranging from
health and welfare to police protection and equal employment
opportunity. Put simply, students of women and politics need
to focus on the local institutions because women have both
much to gain from local involvement and much to lose from
neglect of the local governmental scene.
      Accordingly, two beliefs guide this study: first that while
the local political system significantly impacts on women, it also
affords women greater power and influence relative to other

levels of government; second, that to advance women's movement objectives specific institutions designed to enhance
political power of women must be examined and assessed.   In
conjunction these beliefs prompt a rigorous inquiry into local
Commissions on the Status of Women.   Though viewed by their
proponents inside the women's movement as representing a
successful nationwide effort to institutionalize female participation at the local level, neither the actual nor potential
contribution of these institutions is firmly established.   The
present study was designed to examine the performance of
CSW.   Both the research design itself and the analysis and
interpretation of data are deeply influenced by a recognition of
the limits on the advisory commission as an institution and of
the constraints under which the early presidential and state
Commissions on the Status of Women have operated.

RESEARCH DESIGN AND DATA BASE

As Marilyn Falik notes, feminist scholars implicitly or explicitly
are political activists as well as theorists of social change.(23)
The mark of applied feminist research is that it is both
instrumental in nature and directed toward analyzing how
political institutions might be adapted to further women's
movement objectives.   Such a basic value orientation is a point
of departure for designing this research.
        Performance serves as a framing concept, for it is
sufficiently broad and rich to facilitate both tasks undertaken
by this study: first, to describe Commissions on the Status of
Women as institutional components of the women's movement;
and, second, to assess their potential for serving as institutional levers for change.   A recent work on governmental
performance suggests that the word performance has at least
three connotations in social science research.   Organizational
performance may suggest organizational purposes or what the
organization intends; it may mean organizational impact, the
effect of organizational activity on the environment of the
organization or upon the organization itself; or it may refer
simply to organizational activities, or what the organization
actually does.(24)   These three dimensions of "performance"
serve here as different sides of a prism through which the
actions of Commissions on the Status of Women can be studied
and assessed.
        The research design facilitating this study of commission
performance is both causal and comparative in nature.
Boutilier and Kelly, in writing on methodologies for studying
women and politics, liken this approach to a biographical case
study in that it investigates relationships by observing
existing consequences and searches back through time for

causal factors.(25)   Though clearly ex post facto, this approach differs from biographical research in that more than
one subject is involved.   Thus, the causal comparative design
allows the researcher to go beyond simply "telling the story."
As Boutilier and Kelly stress, "Its main justification is that the
design yields useful information about what might go with
what, under what conditions, and in what sequences and
patterns.(26)

Accordingly, the causal comparative method is especially
appropriate to this study of local Commissions on the Status of
Women.   Here the method frames inquiry into three specific
questions.   First, What are the conditions under which high
performance occurs?   Second, What constitutes and promotes
"performance" for high-performing commissions?   Third, How is
this performance assessed by key constituent groups of local
commissions?

The unit of analysis is the Commission on the Status of
Women itself.   Commissions are studied at both the macro and
micro level, with much more intensive effort directed to the
micro level.   Commission performance is the primary dependent
variable.

At the macro level, to secure an overall perspective on
factors associated with variation in performance, I studied the
population of official governmental commissions in operation in
1975.   (Nongovernmental Commissions on the Status of Women
were not included in this study because of the variety of
shapes and forms they assume.   Four such local commissions
were registered with the Women's Bureau in 1973-74.   Undoubtedly many more operate in communities across the
country.)   Information on the performance and structure of
commissions was coded directly from questionnaires sent by the
Women's Bureau to all commissions operating during the summer
of 1975.   Officially there were 75 local commissions at that
time.   About 60 of these maintained some level of activity; 48
of these functioning commissions returned the questionnaire.
In order to derive profiles of high-performing commissions,
additional information on the political and demographic setting
of each commission was drawn from the City-County Data
Book, 1972, State and Local Government Special Studies: U.S.
Census Bureau, and the Municipal Yearbook, 1973.

This macro-level analysis clearly highlights factors
associated with various dimensions of performance and aids in
isolating that population of commissions from which cases for
in-depth study of "successful" commissions can be drawn.   It
cannot, however, reveal the contextual information essential to
meaningful interpretation of the relationships found.   Genuine
understanding of the potential contribution of commissions can
only be secured through intensive examination of successful
commissions.

Five Commissions

At the micro level, five commissions received intensive study. These five were selected because they were viewed as "effective" commissions by a panel of seven women, all of whom have held positions in organizations where they have been directly concerned with the establishment and promotion of local Commissions on the Status of Women. Each member of the panel was asked, in a telephone interview, a series of questions designed to elicit, first, her impressions of the meaning of "effectiveness" when applied to commissions on women and, second, her nominations of commissions placing in the top five or six according to this definition. While there was some variation in those commission attributes named as signifying effectiveness, there was surprising consensus on which commissions fell into the "most effective" category. Near consensus existed on six commissions as constituting this group; one of these was dropped from the analysis because of its unique governmental setting. (One community was not included in this study because it was viewed by some panel members as closer to a state commission than a local commission in its operation and self-conception.) The survey data supports the panel consensus by indicating high activity levels for these commissions in terms of range of goal activity areas and degree of substantive issue involvement.

A brief description of the characteristics of each commission studied in depth suggests the rather substantial differences in this set of commissions uniformly judged successful. To protect the confidentiality of the commissions and the informants the locations of the five commissions studied in depth are described only in general terms. The fictitious names given to the communities are: Altona, Dodge, Marysville, Onega, and St. George.

Altona

Altona is a southwestern city of about a quarter million. The home of a major university, Altona has a population reflecting the highest and lowest ends of the educational spectrum. Nonwhites constitute about 12 percent of Altona's citizens and the breakdown between blacks and latins is about 50-50. Roughly 10 percent of Altona's families live below the national poverty level. The Commission on the Status of Women in Altona has been established in some form for nearly ten years but within the past five years has undergone substantial revitalization and reorganization. It enjoys little staff support and a negligible, expenses only, budget.

Dodge

Dodge is a large metropolitan county of over a million. Located in the southeast, Dodge's latin population constitutes over a third of the community. Poverty is also evident in Dodge where over ten percent of the families live below the national poverty level. Blacks constitute a substantial minority population in this county. The commission on the Status of Women in Dodge has been operating continually without major reorganization for nearly ten years. It has a moderate level of staff support with an executive director and a secretary. The commission's financial support is disguised in the county budget and has remained modest but consistent over the years.

Marysville

Marysville is an affluent, very highly educated suburban county in the eastern part of the country. A very low percentage of its half million residents live in poverty (under 3 percent) but small pockets of severe poverty do exist. Though nonwhites constitute substantial proportions of the populations of surrounding jurisdictions, Marysville is a largely (95 percent) white community. The commission in this community has been in existence for over seven years and enjoys substantial staff support and a generous budget.

Onega

Onega is a medium-size midwestern city with about 350,000 residents. Less affluent than Marysville, but more financially secure than Altona or Dodge, Onega's percentage of families below the national poverty level is just below 7 percent. The Catholic Church seems to exercise a strong influence in the culture and even politics of this city. The nonwhite population of slightly over 10 percent adds some heterogeneity to this otherwise highly homogeneous midwestern town. Onega's Commission on the Status of Women has been in existence for nearly eight years. Thanks in large part to the gradual budget increases over the past few years, the commission enjoys the benefit of a strong staff with an executive director and several assistants.

St. George

St. George, like Marysville, is a county populated largely by affluent and highly educated people. Located in the west, St. George is a large county of over a million residents. Though its nonwhite population is just over 5 percent, it is largely latin and appears to be a significant political force. The

Commission on the Status of Women in St. George is well
supported by the county. The executive director and her
staff seem to succeed in gaining additional resources when
needed to support the work of this commission which has been
operating for over five years.

Assembling the performance picture for each of these
commissions involved visiting the communities for a period of
from six to nine days. In every community I conducted
interviews with three groups of people: high-level public
officials, leaders of the major women's activist organizations,
and commission leadership and staff.

The public officials included the mayor and/or the chief
executive officer of the jurisdiction, the heads of the human
relations departments or the relevant enforcement official for
the civil rights law in effect, heads of affirmative action
programs, and selected city council or county commission
members. These interviews were generally the shortest,
lasting from 30 to 90 minutes. In each community five officials
were interviewed.

The women's organization activists included women who
were the formal leaders of the major women's organizations in
the community. In each community, where possible, I interviewed the convener of the National Organization for Women
(NOW) (four of five communities), and the president of the
League of Women Voters (LWV). The pool of women activists
was enlarged by asking the NOW and LWV leaders, as well as
commission members, to name the most visible and/or influential
women's activist groups in the community. There was surprising agreement on the groups named within communities,
and in each community this process generated from three to
six additional names of women holding leadership roles in
major local women's groups. Activist leaders interviewed
represented the Business and Professional Women's Association,
American Association of University Women, the Women's Political
Caucus, women's centers, lesbian collectives, the Junior
League, black sororities, local ethnic and/or minority women's
associations, a third-world collective, a peer-counseling
collective, a welfare mothers group, and a women employee
association. These interviews generally lasted from 90 minutes
to two hours.

The commission members interviewed included the executive officers of the commission, plus the chairpersons of all
active task forces or committees. These interviews generally
also lasted from 90 minutes to two hours. The interviews with
the commission executive director and/or other staff were much
longer. The total time spent interviewing staff ranged from
two-and-a-half hours in one commission with only part-time
staff support to seven hours in the more heavily staffed
commissions. From six to ten commission members were interviewed in each community.

The interview schedule employed was pretested in a pilot study conducted in November of 1976. Modifications carried out as a result of that pretest resulted in the final interview schedule shown in Appendix A. Interviews were taped and later transcribed. In those cases where interviewees expressed a desire not to be taped, notes were taken during the interview and written up immediately following the session.

Additional information on the performance of these commissions was procured from careful review of commission documents and records, as well as from personal observation of the CSW in action. Information on how commissioners and staff spent their time was documented for each commission. A personal profile questionnaire, shown in Appendix B, provided information on individual characteristics of commission members. The return rate on the questionnaire ranged from a low of 53 percent of CSW membership to a high of 86 percent, with at least three-fourths of the commissioners responding in four of the five commissions.

SIGNIFICANCE OF THE RESEARCH

The significance of this research is rooted in both normative and empirical theory concerns. From the perspective of empirical theory the design follows Melissa Butler's dictum that "the study of women in politics should be used to broaden and deepen the understanding of what political life is about."(27) While there exists a substantial literature to date on citizen participation at the local level, the lion's share of that work is program linked and relates only tangentially to "women" as a constituent group in local communities.(28) Similarly the empirical work on women and politics, while proliferating in recent years, largely focuses on characteristics of female office holders at the state and national levels.(29) Hence, in bringing a new focus to the study of citizen participation and its institutionalization, this study builds on and enlarges two bodies of empirical theory, one relating to women as political actors, the other relating to citizen participation at the community level more generally. The end of broadening and deepening understanding of political life is thus served.

Equally significant are the normative concerns guiding this study. This project is inspired by a vision of democratic theory that conceives of the "public interest" both in terms of the results of the policy-making process and in terms of participation in that process itself. Put in systems language, a democratic society functions adequately only when it allows for citizen participation on the "input" as well as the "output" ends of the decision-making process.(30) In this light, Commissions on the Status of Women may be viewed as linking

mechanisms through which both forms of action can be secured.   In terms of influencing outcome, local commissions
constitute the major governmental unit designed to promote
interests of women as a constituent group in the community.
But their role may be even more significant in facilitating
female involvement in defining "problems," in exploring
strategies for change, and in providing a forum through which
community women may come to see the relationship between
government action and their own life options.   In sum,
through studying the capacity of Commissions on the Status
of Women to magnify the influence of women in local policy
making and to integrate women into the decision-making
process of local policy systems, this project promises to build
on the existing body of empirical knowledge about women as
participants in the political process as well as about the
community-level participation phenomenon.   Furthermore, from
a normative perspective the research aims to explore the role
commissions play in advancing change toward women's movement objectives and in the process further democratizing our
political system.

Finally, both normative and empirical concerns are
engaged when feminists in other nations reflect on the potential of subnational commissions to embody and articulate
women's interests.   For that international audience this study
offers insight into critical dimensions of commission performance at the community level.

ORGANIZATION

Performance is the central concept framing the entire analysis.
The three meanings of performance sketched above frame the
following chapters.

Chapter 2 reviews the population of local commissions
through the prism of the local politics literature.   While here
performance is operationalized merely in terms of organizational
action, this section does provide, in summary fashion, the
political-demographic-organizational profile of a set of commissions with an apparent capacity for high performance.

Chapters 3 through 5 shift to the in-depth examination of
the five commissions deemed to be high performers.   In an
effort to give meaning to the notion of "high performance,"
chapter 3 explores more intensely two dimensions of commission
action.   The first dimension is that of commission goal activity:
What are the goal activity areas in which these commissions are
working?   The goal area self-definition of commissions provides
their raison d'etre.   The second dimension relates to the issue
agenda of commissions: How do successful commissions rank
substantive issues on the women's rights agenda?   How does

this configuration of priorities vary across communities? Are there issues that all commissions find especially compelling? What accounts for the variation in function and agenda found?

Chapter 4 goes beyond fleshing out the patterns of activity to explore the relationship between commissions and their community clientele. Here commission performance is examined strictly in light of the purposes or agenda promoted. One attractive rationale for commissions maintains that they facilitate agenda building in the women's policy area. Examining congruence between commissioners and women organizational activists on importance assigned to issues provides a convenient means to explore this agenda-building activity. Those issues on which the commissions seem unable to participate in agenda building receive particular attention.

In chapter 5, performance becomes defined in terms of organizational impact with the focus on perceptions of commission effectiveness held by significant commission clientele groups. First the issue of how notions of CSW effectiveness can be defined in relation to the potential clientele groups in the community is discussed. Then analysis turns to the relationship between commission priorities on goal activity areas and activist and official assessment of CSW effectiveness. Characteristics of commissions deemed effective from different official and activist perspectives are described.

Chapter 6 returns to the macro level, exploring the relationship between local Commissions on the Status of Women and the women's movement. Given the environmental, political, and organizational parameters on CSW action detailed above, this analysis considers the relative merit of the positive and negative reviews Commissions on the Status of Women receive. A prime goal here is to develop normative criteria for assessing the commissions' potential for mobilizing women's interests and participation in community politics and for, in the process, advancing women's movement ends.

2 Overview of Organization and Performance

Since the town of Beaver Dam, Wisconsin, appointed the first local Commission on the Status of Women in 1966, the number of commissions has proliferated. Today over 82 cities and counties report such institutions playing a role in local government. A preliminary discussion of the organizational and membership characteristics of these commissions paves the way for the prime focus of this book - an examination of commission performance.

ORGANIZATION

Typically, the impetus for establishing a local commission comes from women occupying leadership roles in women's organizations within the community. While the amount of preplanning and the number of individuals involved varies, all commissions share a common birth experience in their official enactment by a local policy-making institution. The two broad types of enactment documents are executive orders and local ordinances. Executive orders, constituting the authorization for some of the local commissions in 1975, offer the advantage of greater freedom for commissions in defining programs and procedures. Typically, however, commission advocates prefer establishment by ordinance which provides greater promise of continuity and possibly greater resources. In either case the enactment document generally spells out many of the organizational details including size and appointment of membership, staffing arrangements, and reporting procedures.

Commissions vary in size ranging from seven to forty members, with the mayor typically making the appointments

when the authorization is by executive order and a variety of
appointment arrangements holding for statutory commissions.
As a rule these statutory commissions, established by ordinance, follow the local governments' standard procedure for
appointments to citizen commissions. It may mean that the
mayor or chief executive officer will appoint and the city or
county council approve appointments; it may require each
council member to make a certain number of appointments - the
practices vary. In all cases, however, there is a clear
political element involved.

Many local commissions are unstaffed or staffed only
minimally. Just under a third of the commissions (31.3
percent) surveyed in 1975 reported employing executive
directors; only 18.3 percent reported additional nonclerical
staff beyond a single executive director. The location of the
commission in the local government establishes the line of
accountability. Some commissions (29.2 percent) report
directly to the mayor or chief executive officer of the jurisdiction; others (43.8 percent) report directly to the legislative
body (county board, city council, county commission); still
others (16.7 percent) report to an administrative official, such
as a director of a human relations commission, who in turn
reports to the next higher administrative official.

Commissions on the Status of Women generally enjoy
substantial discretion in organizing their internal operations.
Some commissions operate with executive committees; some
do not. Most commissions establish both standing and ad
hoc committees to accomplish their objectives. Some commissions allow noncommission members to serve on commission
committees; others do not. In the absence of a formal
requirement that the commission chair be appointed by a
specific official, commissions tend to elect their chairs by a
simple majority vote. The budget picture for commissions also
varies. While a full 53 percent of the commissions responding
to the survey reported no budget in fiscal year 1975-1976,
those funded commissions reported levels varying from $75 to
$79,000. The median budget for the funded commission was
$16,000.

While the level of support may seem low, local-level
advisory commissions in general enjoy only modest funding.
The sole exception to this rule occurs where the commission
or council also carries legally mandated administrative responsibilities in some area. For example a human relations
commission charged with conducting investigations and
reporting to enforcement agencies on the validity of complaints
of race, sex and other kinds of discrimination will typically
receive a larger budget allocation to support necessary staff.

The image emerging from this analysis of the organizational support for commissions lacking these formal administrative responsibilities suggests that in many cases those

individuals serving on such bodies may be the determinant of its success. Given the scant support available to most Commissions on the Status of Women the burden of "making things happen" falls squarely on the shoulders of the citizen commissioners. Hence the question of who they are becomes important.

It is standard fare on commission enactment documents to call for broad representation from all segments of the community, some even specifying "men," "homemakers," "economically disadvantaged," etc. Table 2.1 reports the percentage of three groups - minorities, men, youth (under 25) - serving on the local commissions surveyed in 1975.

Table 2.1. Percentage of Commissions Reflecting
Different Levels of Group Representation:
Minority, Male, Youth

Percent of Group Representation	Minority (N=45)	Male (N=42)	Youth (N=44)
0	15.6	50.0	70.5
1-10	8.9	14.3	11.4
11-20	20.0	21.4	11.4
21-30	28.9	8.4	0.0
above 31	26.7	4.2	6.3
	100.0	100.0	100.0

As table 2.1 suggests, well over half of the commissions show a minority representation of over 20 percent, while only 15.6 percent have no minority group members. Less than a third of the commissions hold minority membership below the national population average of 11.5 percent. Males fare better in terms of winning commission appointments than we might expect. While half of the commissions surveyed reported no male membership, nearly a third of them report more than 10 percent of their numbers are male. Looking only at the sex and minority status variables, appointing officials in many communities must be taking "broad representation" rule into account. Youth, however, seem to fare less well in terms of commission appointments. Less than 20 percent of the commissions surveyed reported any substantial (over 10 percent) youth involvement.

A second way of describing commission members is in terms of their employment status. The 1975 survey revealed that the majority of commissions (56.8 percent) reported that over two-thirds (67 percent or above) of their membership was employed. The lowest percent membership employed reported was 32 percent.

The sketch drawn by examining this 1975 survey shows commissions tending to represent minorities and men to a surprising degree, tending to downplay youth representation, and tending to reflect strongly the employed community. These commission members work under a variety of organization arrangements but in the main share the constraint of limited budget and staff. With this overview as background we now turn to examine the performance of Commissions on the Status of Women.

PARAMETERS OF PERFORMANCE

The purpose of analyzing data from this survey of all commissions operating in 1975 is to gain general insight into the parameters of high performance. Obviously involved is understanding the conditions under which high performance emerges and sketching the organizational characteristics of commissions achieving this distinction. More specifically, this compilation of information provides the basis for empirically derived profiles of commissions falling into high performer category. Two sets of factors - political system traits and socioeconomic traits, are ecological in kind, and as such they are most usefully read as controlling conditions to be taken into consideration in adjusting one's expectation of commissions operating in different environments. A third set of factors, here labeled organizational traits, are to some degree manipulatable. Obviously, from practical women's movement perspective, attention focuses most intently on manipulatable variables and thus the chapter concludes with some broad observations flowing from consideration of the organizational profiles of high-performing commissions. As well this concluding section calls attention to the most manipulatable aspects of performance.

As noted in chapter 1, a recent work on governmental performance suggests that the word performance has at least three connotations in social science research. Organizational performance may suggest organizational purposes or what the organization intends; it may mean organizational impact, the effect of organizational activity on the environment of the organization or upon the organization itself; or it may refer simply to organizational activities, or what the organization actually does.(1)

In analyzing institutional performance the definition of performance employed must reflect both the stage of research

and the research product desired. Given the stage of
research reflected in this preliminary survey of commissions,
problems arise in applying either the organizational purposes
meaning or the organizational impact meaning. Both "purposes" and "impact" analysis require imposing some normative
criterion for evaluating intentions (purposes) and effectiveness
(impact) of CSWs. Yet imposing such criteria on a commission
which, because of ecological factors, may be unable to even
specify intentions much less engage in action to achieve
them, seems meaningless. For example if this survey were
to reveal that most <u>county</u> commissions never move beyond
the stage of assessing the needs of county women, and
therefore they report only one area of commission activity,
i.e., needs assessment, it is pointless to assess their effectiveness in the full complement of activities characteristic of
successful commissions. Thus, this chapter puts forward the
ecological profiles of commissions most likely to have reached
the stage of being able to sustain these more stringent modes
of performance assessment. Organizational purposes and
organizational impact do become relevant in later chapters
where both notions of performance are applied in the intensive
analysis of five high-performing commissions. But for this
preliminary overview the less restrictive notion of performance
as organizational activity promises to yield the greatest
insight.

The rationale underlying this "organizational activity"
conceptualization of performance is that activity is the key to
governmental capacity and that this capacity can be viewed as
the ability "to affect future states of the system of which a
unit is part."(2) When applied elsewhere this rationale has
led to examining the success of government generally in
mobilizing resources and transforming them into expenditures
as the prime indicator of performance.(3) However, when
performance, as capacity, is applied to the analysis of specific
units of government, such as advisory commissions, the
activity indicator need not be limited strictly to expenditures.
While facility in garnering resources is one meaningful measure
of performance, alone it fails to tell all about capacity for
effecting change. Change can be effected through a number
of operational activities and in multiple issue areas. While
commissions' overall goal may be improvement in the life
opportunity of community women, that comprehensive change
objective translates, in practice, into programmatic goals
reflecting areas of operating activity.(4) For example Commissions on the Status of Women may strive to increase political
participation of women or to educate the public on issues
concerning women each reflecting areas of goal activity.
Thus, the range of goal-activity areas adopted by a particular
commission is a second aspect of commission performance. As
well, change can be effected through pursuing these goal

commitments in a number of different substantive areas such as health, education, and employment. Hence, a third aspect of commission performance relates to scope of commission involvement in substantive issue areas.

Thus, in this preliminary analysis of local Commissions on the Status of Women, performance as capacity to influence future events is conceptualized in terms of the 1) capacity to garner financial resources, as measured by CSW total annual budget; 2) range of goal activity areas, as measured by the reported number of commission operating activities; and 3) scope of involvement in substantive issue areas, as measured by the reported number of issue concerns. Operationally these performance measures were derived as follows.

Among the 48 CSWs surveyed in 1975(5) the total yearly budget figure (1974-75), including all grants and reported in-kind service equivalents, ranged from $0 to $77,170. For purposes of analysis the commissions were grouped into un-budgeted commissions, low-budget commissions ($50-$10,999), moderate-budget commissions $11,000-$24,999), and high-budget commissions ($25,000 and above). High-performing commissions on this criterion numbered five. Similarly, commissions were grouped by the range of goal activity areas in which they engaged. CSWs reported five goal-activity thrusts in the years 1974-75. Their areas of operating activity included 1) educating the public on women's issues, 2) increasing political participation of women, 3) assessing the needs of community women, 4) direct lobbying in an effort to influence local decision making on women's issues and 5) coordinating all of the activity areas listed to improve the life opportunities of minority women specifically. For analytic purposes the narrow-range commission is defined as committed to one of these goal areas, the moderate-range commission is committed to two or three goal areas, and the wide-range commission is committed to four or all of the goal areas named. Eleven CSWs appeared as high performers on this measure. Finally, the scope of issue involvement on the part of Commissions on the Status of Women varies considerably. Of 31 issues mentioned by the totality of commissions surveyed in 1975, commissions reported a degree of involvement ranging from zero issues to seven issues. In this performance analysis a commission is treated as low on scope of substantive issue involvement if it reports involvement in less than three issues. Involvement in three or four issues results in a moderate issue involvement in five to nine substantive issue areas and this survey shows 18 commissions in this category.

While all three of these measures, so defined, tap dimensions of performances as capacity to influence future events, meaningful examination of the correlates of such measures requires determining the degree of relationship between measures. There is no reason, a priori, to assume that the three measures of capacity to influence performance should correlate highly with each other. For a CSW, the capacity to secure a generous budget may reflect successful performance in the internal politics of city/county budget negotiations. While this capacity may correlate with CSW clout on relevant internal women's issues, it as well may be associated with a restricted range of goal activity areas, e.g., a commission's thrust may be toward the single objective of directly shaping affirmative action policy and securing implementation in county or city government. Similarly, a commission may have a very low budget, because of certain environmental constraints, but rely heavily on a large volunteer force to maintain a high level of involvement in a substantive issue salient to the community. In either case, there would be no positive relationship between the different dimensions of performance. The survey data on Commissions on the Status of Women buttresses this conceptual understanding of the distinctness of different dimensions of performance.

Table 2.2 reports the measure of independence for each combination of relationships.

Table 2.2. Measure of Independence* between
Dimensions of Performance

Relationship	Chi Square	Significance Level
Goal activity by issue involvement	7.42	0.12
Goal activity by financial resources	8.37	0.21
Issue involvement by financial resources	5.80	0.45

*While the chi square statistic is intended for use on samples, when used as here on a population it can provide guidance. The size of the statistic, with the significance level can give a rough indication of independence of the measures involved.

Establishing the significance level of 0.05, no significant statistical relationships appear to exist between any two measures of performance. Given the fact that dimensions of performance are distinctive, the question becomes: What factors seem to be associated with variation in each type of performance?

A significant strain in local politics literature focuses on determinants of variations of performance in community political systems. Substantial intellectual energy has gone into combing the local scene for valid empirical predictors of "high performance." The sober conclusion, recently drawn from a critical review of this literature, is that similar determinants of performance are not determinant everywhere. "No single cause or set of causes seems to be responsible for shaping the scope and quality of urban government in all of its varying contexts."(6) In light of this conclusion, hypothesis testing, designed to reveal determinants of performance for Commissions on the Status of Women, is premature. A more fitting analysis would simply construct profiles of CSWs based on systematic examination of the entire set of variables, isolated in the community politics literature, as potential determinants of performance.

Thus we draw on the urban systems literature to construct profiles of those commissions distinguishing themselves by their high performance. The independent variables used are those, identified in that literature, which relate to political system traits and to socioeconomic environment traits. Internal organizational traits less well covered in the broader literature are also included. Table 2.3 lists all of the variables considered and reports the relative means or percentages across levels of performance.(7)

While table 2.3 displays all levels of performance with the corresponding differences in political, socioeconomic and organizational traits, the primary concern in this book is with the high-performance phenomenon. Thus, discussion now turns to traits shared by high-performing commissions.

TRAITS SHARED BY HIGH-PERFORMING COMMISSIONS

Under all three criteria for performance, six distinctive traits tend to characterize the profile of high-performing commissions. (Criterion for inclusion of a trait is that the high-performing mean or percentage must be higher than both the lowest performing group figure and the average figure.) High performers tend to be city, rather than county commissions and tend to be located in communities where the conventional indicator of citizen participation suggests high participation rates. The social environment of these commissions distinguishes itself by a high concentration of community power, with the communities themselves tending to be larger than those hosting lower performing commissions.

In terms of internal organizational traits, high-performing commissions are more likely to be staffed with executive directors. These commissions feel more comfortable than do their less successful counterparts in defining advocacy in their organizational roles.

These six traits present no surprises. Because the city governments have conventionally been the target for political demands, they have been the playing field on which activists have gained experience. Hence, high-performing CSWs are found disproportionately in cities over the historically less responsive counties. Similarly, we would expect political systems where citizen participation, and therefore demand, is high to be generally more responsive in meeting women's demands through a citizen-based group like a Commission on the Status of Women. In terms of political system traits, these findings on the correlates of high performance are consistent with those of Aiken and Alford(8) and others. Furthermore, the finding of high-performing CSWs located in communities with a high concentration of community power is consistent with the relationship between concentration of community power and innovation reported by Aiken and Alford and by Hawley.(9) All other things being equal, we would expect the population to be somewhat larger in communities where high-performing CSWs are found, for a certain critical mass of activist women may be necessary to motivate CSW action.

The internal organizational distinguishing mark of a paid executive director on high-performing commissions is predictable. But beyond this obvious point, it is interesting to note that the relative significance of the executive director role appears to be most important where performance is defined in terms of level of substantive issue involvement. It is reasonable to assume that expanded issue involvement is highly dependent on the collection and funneling of information - a task carried on by an executive director. The basis for the association is not so obvious with regard to the inclusion of advocacy in the role of definition of high-performing commissions. The degree to which advocacy and performance complement one another seems somewhat dependent on the definition of performance employed as illustrated by the correlation between advocacy and each performance measure. The relationship ranges from a high of gamma 0.61 between advocacy and degree of involvement in substantive issues, to a gamma of 0.54 between advocacy and range of functional commitments, to a gamma of 0.27 between advocacy and capacity to garner financial resources. Perhaps a Commission on the Status of Women can only assume an advocacy role once performance is established. But in any case high performance and advocacy clearly complement one another and are certainly not mutually exclusive, a finding which undermines the oft heard thesis that a successful commission must eschew advocacy.

Table 2.3. Internal and External Profiles of Commissions by
Variation in Levels of Performance According to
Three Dimensions of Performance

	Range of Goal Activity Areas				
Profile Traits	Narrow	Moderate	Wide	Group Average	N
Political Traits					
Political culture	3	3.1	3.6	3.2	(39)
Citizen participation[a]	52%	58.2	65%	59.7	(38)
Reform[c]	75%	52%	60%	56.8	(37)
Public regardingness[a]					
(% foreign stock)	15%	17.6	19.2	17.8	(39)
(% children in private school)	19.3%	10.8	9.8	11.2	(38)
Form of election[b]	75%	36.4	27.3	37.8	(37)
Jurisdiction (% city)	25%	45.8	63.6	48.7	(39)
Manager form of government[c]	25%	54.2	45.5	48.7	(39)
Socioeconomic Traits					
Concentration of community power[a]	24%	25.7	30.4	27	(38)
Community Integration[a]	5%	4.2	4.4	4.3	(38)
Size of community[a]	176,086	361,782	391,594	351,145	(39)
Poverty[a]	9%	8.9	7.2	8.4	(39)
Racial composition[a] (% nonwhite)	12%	13.4	20.6	15.5	(37)
Constituency need[a] (% women head of household)	14%	12%	12%	12%	(38)
Internal Organizational Traits					
Size of membership	12.8	17.3	16	16.8	(39)
Staff support (% with executive director)	33.3%	30.4	40	33.3	(36)
Location (% in the executive branch)	33.3%	27.3	40	31.4	(35)
Advocacy perspective (% advocates)	25%	16.7	54.5	28.2	(39)
Tenure (data established)	72.5	72.7	72.1	62.7	(39)

Sources: (a) City-County Data Book, 1972.
          (b) State and Local Government, Special Studies #68, table 5, U.S. Bureau
               of Census.
          (c) Municipal Year Book, 1973.

Continued

Scope of Issue Involvement					Capacity to Garner Resources					
Low	Moderate	High	Average	N	No Budget	$30-$10,999	$11,000-$24,999	$25,000 or above	Average	N
2.7	4	3.3	3.2	(48)	3.3	3.3	3.1	3.2	3.3	(48)
56.3%	61.2	60.4	59.2	(45)	55%	58.7	60.3	68.8	59.2	(45)
37.5%	63.6	64.7	54.5	(44)	72.7%	38.1	71.4	60	54.5	(44)
15.2%	18.6	19	17.6	(46)	14.1%	19	15.9	22.2	17.6	(46)
10.6%	11.6	11.2	11.2	(45)	10.6%	11.4	12.1	10	11.2	(45)
20%	63.6	47.1	41.9	(43)	45.5%	40	57.1	20	41.9	(43)
50%	41.7	55.6	50	(48)	25%	58.3	42.9	80	50	(48)
29.4%	58.3	55.6	46.8	(47)	58.3%	39.1	43.9	60	46.8	(47)
25.4%	27.9	27.8	26.8	(45)	24.5%	26.5	28	33.4	27	(45)
4.4%	4.3	4.2	4.3	(45)	4.7%	4.1	3.9	5.2	4.3	(45)
178,527	319,742	931,947	510,182	(46)	270,529	647,917	437,869	580,554	510,182	(46)
8.9%	8.8	8.2	8.6	(46)	9.8%	8.5	8.4	6.2	8.6	(46)
11.3%	11.4	20	14.6	(45)	17.4%	14.3	16.3	8.2	14.6	(45)
10.5%	12.3	12.9	11.7	(45)	13.1%	11.2	13.4	10	11.9	(45)
16.7	16.2	17.5	16.9	(46)	17.3%	18	15.6	12.6	16.9	(46)
17.6%	18.2	62.5	34.1	(44)	20%	18.2	85.7	60	34.1	(44)
37.5%	18.2	37.5	32.6	(43)	40%	28.6	14.3	60	32.6	(43)
5.6%	33.3	38.9	25.0	(48)	16.7%	25	14.3	60	25	(48)
72.4	72.9	72.6	72.6	(46)	72.3	72.5	73.6	72.6	72.6	(46)

TRAITS UNRELATED TO VARIATION IN
COMMISSION PERFORMANCE

Three of the traits examined appear to be associated similarly
with commissions performing at different levels, and hence fail
to uniquely characterize high-performing commissions.   Variations in the political culture of the host community, in the
degree of public regardingness of the political environment and
the age of the commission do not correlate in any systematic
way with high performance.   These findings of no relationship
are interesting for they challenge some of our conventional
wisdom about settings favorable to citizen participation more
generally.

From the literature on political culture we might have
expected CSWs to be more numerous and high performers more
plentiful in communities where the predominant culture is
moralistic and thus supportive of citizen participation and issue
politics.   However, the cosmopolitan orientation of the women's
movement, coupled with the active intervention of national-level
forces (Women's Bureau and the National Association of Commissions on the Status of Women) may have simply smoothed out
some of the undulation that is otherwise produced by variation
in political culture.

Public regardingness is a second variable which might
predictably be associated with the effective expression of
citizen concern channeled through advisory commissions.
Communities where citizens are oriented toward acting on and
shaping their political world would seem fertile ground for
high-performing commissions.   The data is contradictory but
clearly does not support this thesis.   Commission performance
on all three performance measures is negatively associated with
one of the two standard measures of public regardingness,
percent of foreign stock.   On the second measure, percent of
children in private elementary and high schools, the relationship is positive on two measures of performance and
negative on the third.   These mixed results suggest no
relationship that lends itself to meaningful interpretation,
effectively eliminating public regardingness as a distinctive
element in the profile of high-performing commissions.

Age of a commission seems intuitively as if it should be
associated with high performance.   Time is required to build a
power base for garnering resources, to develop a capacity for
operating in a wide range of goal areas, and to carry out
program activities in a large number of substantive issue
areas.   In the case of Commissions on the Status of Women,
however, the periodic election of new appointing officials is a
great leveler.   Since the charters of most commissions allow
the newly elected public official(s) room for influencing commission direction, the attribute of long tenure has not been
particularly advantageous.

TRAITS ASSOCIATED WITH SINGLE DIMENSIONS
OF PERFORMANCE

As noted above the three dimensions of performance are not highly correlated. Thus some attention must be given to those traits that are uniquely associated with only certain dimensions of performance. Since direct interpretation of these relationships is uncertain in light of the low N, especially in the absence of contextual understanding of the communities involved, the empirical subprofiles for each dimension of performance will simply be presented as suggesting hypotheses meriting testing in a richer context.

Performance as Range of Goal-Activity Areas

Communities hosting CSWs that score high on this performance criterion tend to elect some or all of their county/city council members from districts or wards. The communities themselves tend to be more affluent, yet tend to have a higher nonwhite population than do commissions lower on this dimension of performance. In terms of CSW structure, a larger proportion of commissions high on this dimension of performance are located in executive offices, rather than under legislative bodies or administrative agencies.

Performance as Scope of Involvement in Substantive Issues

Commissions on the Status of Women that are high performing on the degree of involvement in substantive issues are more often found in reform-oriented political systems than are other commissions. More specifically these high performers tend to be located in nonpartisan electoral systems where the local legislative officials are elected at large, and where the local governments operate under the council manager system. In terms of social environment, the degree of social needs, as inferred by the percent of women heads of households, is higher for these high-performing commissions than for their lowering performing counterparts. The one organizational characteristic, uniquely distinguishing these high performers is their relatively larger size.

Performance as Capacity to Garner Resources

Commissions that exhibit a strength in garnering financial resources tend to appear in jurisdictions electing their local legislative officials from districts rather than at large and thus

to some extent their political systems suggest a nonreform
tradition. Features of the socioeconomic environment of these
CSWs include a tendency to be somewhat lower on community
integration as measured by percent unemployment. At the
same time the degree of poverty, the degree of racial parity,
and the degree of social need are significantly lower than are
those percentages for the lesser performing commissions. Size
of CSW membership distinguishes high-performing commissions
on the resource dimension, but unlike in the case described
above, where high-performing commissions were larger than
their less successful counterparts, high-performing CSWs in
this case are smaller in membership.

COMMISSION PROFILES: THEIR APPLICATION

These empirically derived profiles of commissions have a trifold
value. Of course, from a broad disciplinary perspective such
straightforward examination of the correlates of performance
contributes to our cumulative understanding of sources of
performance variation in the local setting. Equally significant
from a women's movement perspective it highlights internal
organizational factors that, within certain political and socioeconomic settings, may facilitate high performance for CSW.
Finally it reveals that "performance" defined as capacity to
influence future events is a complex phenomenon in which
dimensions seemingly vary independent of level of CSW
funding.
    One principal rationale for feminist scholarship in this
area is to better understand how to utilize institutions at the
local level. This rationale fits neatly with the applied social
science dictum - to pursue most intensely those phenomena
most susceptible to manipulation. This chapter concludes with
focus on two such manipulatable phenomena, considering first
the organizational profile of high-performing commissions and
second the distinction between dimensions of performance.
    Lacking information about the nature of the interaction
between manipulatable organizational variables and the more
intractable traits of the political system and socioeconomic
environment, what rough guidelines for organizational con-
struction of Commissions on the Status of Women merit
consideration within the context of individual decision settings?
It appears that, in accordance with our expectations, commissions with paid executive directors have a greater capacity
for performance than do all-volunteer commissions. Less
consistent with the preconceptions of some is the fact that
eschewing advocacy is not a prerequisite of high performance.
The fact that a markedly higher percentage of high-performing
commissions perceived the role of the commission as "advocate

for women's rights" suggests that natural compatibility rather than conflict prevails. For the commission that aspires to engage in a large number of programmatic goal activities, location of the CSW under the chief executive officer seems the most promising spot. However, the location of the commission in the governmental structure has little impact on the scope of commission involvement in substantive issues. In terms of the number of substantive issues with which a commission is involved, commission size may be an important factor in high performance. Commissions with larger memberships appear to have the capacity for involvement in a larger scope of substantive issues. The converse, however, appears to be true when performance is defined in terms of capacity for acquiring financial resources. Commissions with smaller membership have a higher capacity for acquiring greater financial resources.

What is suggested by these profiles is not proof of the determinants of performance in any sense, rather simply the association between organizational structures and measures of performance. It is clear, however, that on the performance side some dimensions are more amenable to CSW action than others.

Of the three performance dimensions discussed here, range of activities and intensity of issue involvement are undoubtedly more susceptible to CSW initiative than is the budget measure. This point is particularly well illustrated by the responses commissions gave to a request put to them by the Women's Bureau in 1975: "Describe briefly any serious problems faced by your commission in areas such as funding, administration, programs, other." The majority of the commissions named funding. Even the executive director of a relatively well-funded commission in a large metropolitan area responded: "Year to year the Commission faces uncertainties as to funding. . . . Uncertainties over timing and amounts of appropriations pose difficulties in the retention of support staff." However, many commissions acknowledge their budget problems to be part of the difficulty faced by all citizen advisory boards and many agencies and express little optimism for dramatic changes occurring in budgeting levels.

If in fact the limitation on financial resources is perceived as a fairly consistent constraint across communities, then budget variation, up or down, while surely an indicator of capacity for performance, may be less significant for applied purposes. It is from this vantage point that the other two aspects of performance - range of goal activities and scope of issue involvement - are deemed especially worthy of in-depth study. Chapter 3 provides a fuller picture of the content of these two aspects of performance and describes the context producing variation within them.

3 Successful Commissions: Goal-Area Activities and Issue Priorities

In studying Commissions on the Status of Women both their substantive issue concerns and their areas of goal activity merit greater examination. While certain political, socioeconomic, and organizational traits seem associated with variation in performance on these measures, the operationalization of high performance in such terms remains crude. Understanding the meaning of CSW performance calls for more precise information on how commissions both define their goal activity areas and establish issue priorities. This fuller elaboration of performance as well could illuminate contextual forces shaping these goal-area and issue-priority choices.

Guided by the gaps in the preceding overview of commission performance this chapter examines the relative importance of various types of goal activities and the priority assigned to different substantive issues for a set of high-performing commissions. The earlier overview focused on goal activities and issue priorities as a way of distinguishing between successful and unsuccessful commissions. This micro analysis fills in the content of "performance" first through examining a set of particularly successful commissions and then by probing the "context" factors explaining variation found in the content of performance for that set of commissions.

Grasping the meaning of performance in terms of the goal activity of Commissions on the Status of Women first requires clarifying the relationship of the phrase "goal activity" to "organizational goal." What is an organizational goal and how do we operationalize it in terms of activities of Commissions on the Status of Women? Lawrence Mohr in his bibliographical review of the organizational goal concept notes that "Common usage, as indicated by all leading dictionary definitions, suggests that goal is an intent to achieve some outcome."(1) From an organizational perspective a goal is such an intent,

collectively held. Group or organizational goals are those held
collectively by members for the group as an entity.(2) In
direct application to a specific organization, an organizational
goal becomes, according to Etzioni, "a desired state of affairs
which the organization attempts to realize."(3) The definition
thus can be broken down into three component parts. First
there is the desire on the part of the organization to achieve
some outcome - or the intent; second, there is the organizational attempt to achieve that outcome - or the goal activity;
third, there is the desired state of affairs itself, the condition
to be achieved - the referent.(4) The second component part
preoccupies the goal analysis in this chapter, but a word
about each component places this goal-activity analysis in
proper perspective.

In the five commissions studied in depth the intent of
Commissions on the Status of Women is straightforward and
highly abstract. (See the interview schedule, Appendix A.)
In response to the question: "What would you say is the
overall goal of the Commission on the Status of Women in your
community?" commissioners' responses are highly generalized.
Typical responses are:

> "To improve the status of women: whatever it
> takes to get it done."
> "To speak to the problems and issues of women
> in this country."
> "We don't really say it like this but I think the
> commission goal is to change things for the better-
> ment of women."
> "I think to represent the interests of women in
> the community."

An earlier study of CSWs in the Washington, D.C. metropolitan area similarly reported commissioner goals as being
general, broad and idealized.(5)

Such idealized goals may frame the activities of Commissions on the Status of Women in all communities and provide
the rationale for assessing commissions' agenda building as
addressed in the next chapter. However they tell us little
about what commissions actually do. Focusing on the second
component of Etzioni's goal definition, the organizational
attempt to achieve some specific outcome, generates information
about specific goal activities. Only through understanding the
nature of these activities and the constraints limiting their
realization can we ultimately assess the relative performance of
commissions in terms of the "resultant" - the third component
of Etzioni's goal analysis and chapter 5 will address this latter
component by examining the extent to which observers deem
the desired conditions attained.

Here we focus simply on the concept of goal activity. Goal activity constitutes the means through which organizations attempt to achieve their "intended states of affairs." Performance can only be elaborated in terms of this goal activity. Recognizing that goal activity is multiple, i.e., there are many types of goal activities directed toward commission goals, it is necessary to determine empirically the general set of goal activities characteristic of Commissions on the Status of Women. After defining the goal activities commonly pursued by commissions, we can turn to consideration of factors affecting differences in this pattern of goal activities.

GOAL-AREA ACTIVITY: GENERAL OVERVIEW

The first Presidential Commission on the Status of Women (PCSW) shaped in varying degrees the means by which succeeding commissions attempted to attain their goal of improving the status of women. When state CSWs were established in response to the national call, the institutions that emerged across the states manifested a striking resemblance to one another. For the most part they proceeded, as did the presidential commission, to study the needs of women and to recommend policy action to the relevant legislature and executive officials. Nothing in the history of early state commissions belies the conventional wisdom on governments' motivation for establishing such citizen groups. Daniel Bell, an analyst of the presidential advisory commission as an institution, summarizes this wisdom as follows: 1) to provide a means for the representation of functional constituencies in the advisory process, 2) to permit government to explore informally the limits of action by taking samples in various bodies, 3) to serve as a direct public relations device to call support for various policies, and 4) to foster "elite" participation in the formation of government policy.(6) The Handbook for Commissions on the Status of Women, focusing primarily on state CSWs, once enumerated a list of activity areas that fit well with this interpretation of the appointing bodies' motivation. The handbook instructs commissioners on promoting the appointment of women to boards and commissions, on carrying out public education, on directly influencing the policy-making process, and on modes of conducting needs assessments.(7)

In the early days of state Commissions on the Status of Women, few commissions went beyond this prepackaged understanding of their roles. The highly political character of appointments to state CSWs, the enormous difficulty of independently thinking through indigenous roles for commissions convening infrequently, and the dearth of staff available

to initiate and implement new departures, generally combined
to freeze the conception of state CSW goal activity in the
presidential commission mold.

For a variety of reasons, local commissions appear, in
part, to have escaped the heavy hand of this tradition. In
the first place, strong emphasis on policy recommendation
makes less sense at the local level, since many of the key
decisions impacting locally are made in the state or federal
arenas. Furthermore, since local commissions came into being
after their state counterparts, key figures in their establishment had ample opportunity to observe the operations of the
state commission and, with that model in mind, to speculate on
a broader spectrum of means to achieve the objective of
improving the condition of women locally. In addition,
groundwork preliminary to advancing policy recommendations
often had been done by state CSWs in a form which facilitated
direct local use of the data, thus obviating the requirement for
needs assessment in some areas. Finally, the initiative for the
establishment of local commissions tended to come from a wider
range of viable women's activist groups than had the initiative
for state commissions. (In most states the Business and
Professional Women's Association was the major activist group
behind establishing a state CSW.) All of these factors
contributed to an expanded set of goal activities tackled by
local Commissions on the Status of Women as they grew in
number through the early 1970s.

Review of recent Women's Bureau surveys of local
commissions, coupled with information generated by a pilot
study of one successful commission led to the delineation, in
the five communities studied, of seven goal-activity areas for
local Commissions on the Status of Women. A brief description
of each of these areas provides a background for examining
the pattern of local commission activity.

(On the Women's Bureau survey, which was the basis for
the macro-level analysis, five categories were used to code
goal activity information. The categories were drawn from
national associations' definition of the CSW function, plus the
minorities' concerns function named by the Women's Bureau.
The pilot study of successful CSWs revealed slightly different
functions were most appropriate to local CSWs. Dropped was
the distinct "minority-related" goal activity; watchdog/
analytical, convener/catalyst, and direct support services
were included.)

Public Education

Commissions strive to raise the level of awareness in the community regarding problems women confront. The target group
here might be women themselves, as in the case of a workshop
on "Women and Insurance" designed to disseminate information

to women about the strengths and weaknesses of various
kinds of insurance programs. Public education in this case
aims to provide female members of the community specific
information which might be used to improve their individual life
chances in a fairly specific fashion. On the other hand a
commission's public education activities might be directed to
the community at large, as in the case of a series of public
service announcements on the rights and responsibilities of all
parties to a credit or lending transaction. Here the commission attempts to heighten total community awareness of
current inequities in the system and to inform borrowers and
lenders of existing legal or other avenues for redress.

Needs Assessment

Commissions attempt to determine the major needs felt by
women in the community. Activities supporting this thrust
might include conducting community-wide or more narrowly
targeted surveys, analyzing previously collected community
demographic data, and holding either community-wide or
targeted public hearings, sometimes called "speak out" con-
ferences, which encourage women to report on their own
needs. A commission may view this activity as gathering
ammunition necessary in motivating service agencies to action.
Commissions frequently use such data to set their own programmatic objectives and subsequently to lobby for resources
required to move toward those objectives.

Watchdog/Investigative

Commissions may monitor the implementation of various federal,
state, or local statutes designed to promote equal opportunity
for women. Activities within this context might include the
Commission on the Status of Women assuming a leadership role
in a city or county affirmative action committee. It may lead
to involvement in the implementation of Title IX of the Education Act of 1972 which prohibits discrimination in public school
programming. It could manifest itself in supervising compliance either with Title VII of the Civil Rights Act of 1964, the
federal statute banning sex discrimination in employment, or
with a local fair-employment practice ordinance specifically
covering local industry. The objective in each of these cases
would be to bring the community institutions into compliance
with the relevant laws through institution-level intervention.
This type of goal activity should be distinguished from the
individual case work which fits under direct support services,
although there is clearly a close relationship between the two.

Expansion of Political Participation of Women

Commissions often work to increase the numbers of women in positions of power in local government. Activities supporting this objective would include the maintenance and active utilization of a data bank on women qualified for appointment to boards and commissions, effectiveness training for women interested in public roles, and systematic recruitment of women to serve on CSW task forces and subcommittees. The objective here ranges from the instrumental one of facilitating the appointment of more women, presumed to represent women's interests in important decision-making bodies, to the more expressive one of enlarging the number of opportunities for women to act out their political selves through public participation.

Direct Influence in Policy Making

Commissions frequently strive to shape the outcome of policy making at the local, state, or federal level through some form of direct intervention. Intervention may occur as commissioners lobby specific elected officials on measures before a legislative body. It may occur in the form of testifying before those legislative committees considering measures affecting women. It may simply involve mounting a letter-writing campaign on an issue before the city or county council, the state legislature, or even Congress. The objective here is straightforward: to secure a policy enactment consistent with the CSW-defined understanding of women's interests.

Convener/Catalyst

Commissions on the Status of Women often bring together individuals and groups with shared concerns about particular problems faced by community women. The commission's purpose is to ignite action on behalf of those concerned. For example, a commission might convene a meeting of representatives from feminist, human services, and traditional volunteer organizations to discuss in general terms the problem of battered women in the community. Typically such a group then forms a study committee on battered women in order to generate an even broader community-wide response to the problem. The commission might continue to participate as one member of the committee, or it might remain involved only long enough to insure an ongoing programmatic response. In another instance a commission might secure a grant to develop and operate a rape crisis program, but as soon as the program becomes established steps would be taken to make it autonomous. The objective in each of these cases is to generate community support for programmatic action in specific need areas, while maintaining a posture of limited commission involvement.

Direct Support Services

Some commissions directly provide certain services which community women need. The type of such services varies. In some cases commissions strive to provide very general support as in consciousness-raising and assertiveness training seminars; in others they aim to remedy rather specific problems, with for example their self-defense courses or domestic relations legal clinics. Such a service thrust might include individual "stress" counseling aimed at a multitude of problems ranging from domestic violence to discrimination on the job. In addition a commission may define handling complaints as part of its task which in some cases would involve mediating grievances with employers.

Goal-Activity Priorities

All five Commissions on the Status of Women studied in depth reported some concern with each activity area. Still, organizations, particularly successful ones, inevitably assign priorities to their intermediate goals and stress different areas of activity accordingly. The actual configuration of goal-activity priorities for these five successful commissions further illuminates this goal-activity dimension of performance. These rank orderings are based on responses to a question asking the commission leadership in each community to assign an importance score ranging from 5 (of top importance) to 1 (of no importance) to each of the goal-activity areas outlined above. (See interview schedule, question 7, Appendix A.) This commission leadership group included the officers of the commission, the major task force chairpersons and the executive director. The relative importance of these seven goal-activity areas for each individual commission is derived by averaging the responses of this leadership group. Table 3.1 presents the rank orderings of goal activities summarizing the responses of the five commissions.

Table 3.1 suggests that, true to the Presidential Commission on the Status of Women tradition, the commission activity areas of educating the public and directly shaping the outcome of a policy decision remain top priorities for this set of local CSWs. The relatively low priority assigned to needs assessment and the expansion of political participation departs from the presidential commission tradition, but it is understandable in light of both the passage of time and level of government involved. By 1976-77, substantial needs assessment had been conducted at the state level in most states. If

Table 3.1. Summary of CSW Rank Ordering on
Importance of Goal-Activity Areas

Rank	Function	Mean*
1	Public education	4.39
2	Direct influence	4.19
3	Watchdog/investigative	3.90
4	Convener/catalyst	3.52
5	Needs assessment	3.39
6	Expansion of political participation	3.19
7	Direct support services	2.25

*Based on a 1-to-5 scale with each activity area scored individually by commission leadership and professional staff; mean of mean scores for each commission provided.

local commissions employ such data this obviously lessens the requirement for needs assessment. Political participation, in a relative sense, ranks low among the activity areas for local commissions. In part this may be related to the fact that participation opportunity has always been greater for women at the local level than at other levels of government; thus the rationale for stressing participation per se is less compelling than it might be, especially as compared to the national level.(8)

Clearly two new goal-activity areas emerge as relatively high in the role definition of local Commissions on the Status of Women. The watchdog/investigative and the convener/catalyst areas, both unknown in the earlier state commissions, are particularly well suited to the local setting. The watchdog/investigative activity is fostered wherever citizen boards enjoy fairly immediate access to those institutions charged with implementing mandates prohibiting sex discrimination. Such access is more easily attained, and the results or nonresults of compliance on the part of the institution more easily gauged, at the local level than on the state level. In terms of the convener/catalyst activity it seems clearly easier to catalyze activity in an area where the subjects for this action are known and where the problems ripe for catalyst action are apparent. Because the local commission can know its community, both in terms of group interests readied for tapping and issues ripe for action, it is in a better position than its state counterpart to move in this activity area.

Finally these summary rankings confirm that, on the whole, commissions are not highly committed to the direct support services activity area - a finding which blends with common sense preconceptions of the advisory commission role. Though most active commissions do go beyond the strict advisory notion of their roles, they generally feel that heavy commitment to direct provision of services would drain them and ultimately render them incapable of effective action in any of the other goal-activity areas.

This summary presentation of the areas in which local commissions are active and the relative importance assigned that activity for this set of commissions is useful for what it tells us about the general role that local CSWs play, the new areas of activity they are developing, and the threads which continue from their state and presidential counterparts. Still these summary scores disguise much explanation for the priority rankings. Gaining deeper understanding of the sources of the goal-activity thrusts necessitates a look at priorities within each CSW as well. Before turning to this comparative case analysis, however, a second dimension of performance - the general issue orientation of these commissions - requires attention. This summary of substantive issues concerning commissions provides a second basis for assessing CSW performance and its contextual correlates.

ISSUE INVOLVEMENT: GENERAL OVERVIEW

Issue involvement is another way to look at performance. The goal-activity areas discussed above refer to choices commissions make about general strategies for improving the condition of community women. Commissions act out these strategies through involvement in substantive issues. This analysis focuses intitially on a general overview of the priorities assigned by commissions to activity in a large number of substantive issue areas.

The population of substantive issues studied was drawn primarily from the national women's agenda.(9) The 11 items and 75 subitems appearing on that agenda were melded into a list of 20 substantive issues put in terms commonly identifiable across communities studied. In each interview conducted, respondents were given the opportunity to add issues that were not included on the list; none of the four additional issues named was mentioned in more than one community.

Given what we know about the workings of pluralist politics in America, we would expect the major substantive focus of these successful CSW to be on 1) issues that are resolvable within the constraints of the existing social/economic/legal framework, and 2) issues that, if controversial, have been raised elsewhere in a form that government can't ignore. In this latter case an advisory commission functions as a lightning rod to draw heat from elected public officials.(10) Those women's policy issues most resolvable within the constraints of the existing framework of political consciousness are the bread-and-butter issues - equal employment, education and training, child care, health care, etc. The least resolvable issues within this same political consciousness are the more personal ones such as sexual preference, self-assertiveness, and abortion. Past practices of advisory commissions in general lead to the expectation that excepting cases where the local officials want to use the commission to diffuse an explosive issue, the Commissions on the Status of Women will tend to give priority to those problems for which remedies are clearly available within the current political consciousness.

Table 3.2, exhibiting the averaged priority ranks for the five commissions studied, offers an opportunity for exploring this thesis. As with goal-activity priorities, the issue priorities for each commission are ascertained by asking commission leadership to assign an importance score ranging from 5 (of top importance) to 1 (of no importance) to each of the issues drawn from the national women's agenda. Again, the commission leadership group included the officers of the commission, chairpersons of major task forces and the executive director. The relative importance of these 20 issues for each individual commission is derived by averaging the responses of this leadership group. Table 3.2 presents a priority list based on the average of these averages.

This summary of CSW judgment about the relative importance of 20 substantive issues confirms in part that CSW are likely to manifest high concern with bread-and-butter issues. Three of the top five issues are classic issues of this type: child care, education and training, and employment. A closer look at the data, however, suggests an alternative descriptive category. The common element in the top five issues is that in a very basic sense they are all survival issues. Comments made by CSW members buttress this point. Battered women and rape are distinguished from the other three issues merely in terms of the numbers of women affected. By way of contrast none of the five lowest ranked issues were generally perceived as "survival" issues by commissions in any of the communities. To say this is not to say that housing, for example, may not be a survival issue to a homeless female head of household. Rather it simply suggests that the CSW

Table 3.2.   Summary of CSW Rank Ordering on
             Importance of Issues(a)

Rank	Issue	Mean Score
1	Employment	4.191
2	Child care	4.088
3	Rape	4.082
4	Battered women	4.058
5	Education and training	3.845
6	ERA	3.666
7	Credit	3.574
8	Legal rights/marriage and family	3.570
9	Media	3.566
10	Ethnic/minority condition	3.434
11	Self-assertiveness	3.099
12	Health care	3.070
13	Female offenders	3.005
14	Political participation(b)	2.953
15	Insurance	2.885
16	Housing	2.683
17	Family planning	2.491
18	Abortion	2.477
19	Tax law	2.142
20	Sexual preference	1.366

(a)   The table reflects only those 20 issues which all CSW
members were asked to respond to.   The four issues added
were not "issues" in all of the communities and thus not
included in this summary ranking.
(b)   Political participation can be treated as an issue or goal-
activity area.

members did not perceive it as such. The general perception was that these lowest priority issues, three of which are highly personal issues, posed no problems of survival for women in the community.

This discussion of commission issue orientations, together with the earlier description of their goal activities, provides an overview of the content of commission performance. From this overview we can draw a general sense of the pattern of issue involvement and the direction of goal activity of successful commissions. However, in attempting to isolate those factors associated with differences in the pattern of performance, whether as goal activity or issue orientation, a comparative examination of the context in which these patterns are formed provides great insight. Now we begin to examine that context in each of the communities.

CONTEXT FACTORS: POLITICAL SOURCES OF VARIATION IN CSW PERFORMANCE

As an actor in American politics the Commission on the Status of Women falls between two types of institutions. On the one hand, it shares with community action groups the characteristic of both representing a specific constituency and advocating the interests of that constituency. On the other hand, it is established as an advisory board, organizationally responsible to and dependent upon the local unit of government. Hence in surveying the literature for contextual factors capable of explaining variation in forms of commission actions, research on both advisory commissions and community action groups becomes relevant. A review of each of these literatures produces the set of factors, reflecting the potential sources of variation in commission performance. Table 3.3 displays the main variables, labeled context characteristics, along with their primary analytical components.

Given this set of characteristics how might we describe the contextual correlates of the different priorities assigned goal activities and substantive issues by these successful commissions? Focusing first on the goal activities, table 3.4 documents the differences apparent across the five communities studied. Next each goal-activity area is discussed in terms of the contextual factors associated with the difference in the importance assigned to this goal activity across communities.

Public Education

Public education has long been recognized as a central function of advisory commissions in general and Commissions on the

Table 3.3.   Context Characteristics Relevant to CSW
Goal Activities and Issue Agenda

Characteristics of Context	Analytical Component	
Membership characteristics	1. Age	7. Income
	2. Sex	8. Marital status
	3. Race	9. Education
	4. Religion	10. Party activism
	5. Party identity	11. Women's movement activism
	6. Occupation	12. Interest
Organizational characteristics	1. Authorization	
	2. Size of CSW	
	3. Size of staff	
	4. Interorganizational setting	
	5. Appointment procedures - CSW	
	6. Appointment procedures - staff	
	7. Formal location of decision-making authority	
	8. Distribution of commission/staff control	
	9. Number of committees	
	10. Control procedure for committees	
	11. Control procedure for executive service	
	12. Age of CSW	
	13. Formal goal statement	
Resources	1. Amount of appropriation, grant, in-kind services	
	2. Source of organization, grant, in-kind services	
Community background	1. Sources of support	
	2. Circumstances that bring about establishment	
	3. Breadth of support	
	4. Structure of support	
Governmental responsiveness	1. Responsiveness of bureaucracy	
	2. Responsiveness of decision-making/appointing officials	

Source: Derived from the outline of group characteristics reflecting significant variation in a report by the Urban Studies Group, Citizen Participation Group: A Report to the National Urban Observatory (Lawrence: University of Kansas, 1970); and Elrud Harari, "Japanese Politics of Advice in Comparative Perspective: A Framework for Analysis and a Case Study," Public Policy 22 (Fall 1974): 537-77.

Table 3.4.   Rank Ordering on Importance of
Goal Activity: All Commissions

		Commissions		
Goal Activity	Marysville (N=7)	Onega (N=8)	Dodge (N=9)	Altona (N=6)	St. George (N=9)
Public education	1	2	2.5	1	1
Needs assessment	4	7	6	3.5	6
Watchdogging	3	4.5	4.5	2	3
Expand participation	6	4.5	4.5	6	5
Direct influence policy	2	1	1	5	2
Convener/catalyst	7(a)	3	2.5	3.5	4(b)
Direct services	5(c)	6(b)	7(d)	7	7(b)

(a)   N=6
(b)   N=7
(c)   N=2
(d)   N=8

Status of Women in particular. To be sure some observers have taken the jaundiced view that "public persuasion" might better describe these pedagogical functions of advisory commissions.(11)   Some antifeminists, with an equally disapproving eye, have interpreted this public education commitments as taxpayer-subsidized "brainwashing." Nonetheless, from the perspective of many CSW members, public education is the cornerstone on which all else is built. Typically commission members report, "If the public . . . is aware . . . the rest of it all becomes much more easy," and "Public education is the basis of everything."

Not all commissions, however, rate public education as the top-priority activity area. Two organizational characteristics, membership size and formal goal statement of the commission, distinguish the three commissions that award public education this rating. These three CSW (Marysville, Altona, and St. George) have a membership of 15 or under as opposed to the

substantially larger commissions of 26 and 40 in Onega and
Dodge, respectively. One could speculate that whereas a more
conscious effort must be taken to advance the education
objective in the case of the smaller CSWs, commissions with
large memberships perform public education activities naturally
through the extended network of task forces designed to keep
all involved. Because public education does not "just happen"
the smaller commission may feel compelled to stress public
education as a goal-activity area.

However, given the propensity across all commissions to
report that "education is the key to everything," a more
compelling explanation for the relative deemphasis of education
in Onega and Dodge resides in the formal goal statement of the
commission. The designation of public education as a CSW goal
area is absent from the enactment documents of Onega and
Dodge County, the two commissions ranking this function as
less than top priority. Clearly, it is difficult to place as the
number-one priority an area of activity that was not even
mentioned in the enabling documents. St. George County,
Marysville County, and Altona were all created by documents
specifically naming "public education" as inherent in the CSW
role.

Direct Influence on the Policy Process

As with public education, direct influence on the policy-making
process tends to rank as one of the top two priorities. The
desire to develop a mechanism for directly influencing decision
making in local government motivated the establishment of
Commissions on the Status of Women, being named as a major
element in all of the enabling documents. Altona distinguishes
itself from the other CSW by giving an overall low ranking of
fifth place to the direct influence activities. Organizational
factors apparently interact with governmental responsiveness to
explain this difference.

Exercising direct and ongoing influence on the policy
process requires a certain degree of institutionalization. An
advisory unit must become in some way part of the policy-
making process in order to influence it. This can be done
through a politically sapient executive director or, to a lesser
extent, through stable and highly institutionalized task forces
or committees that persist until they insinuate themselves into
the policy-making process. Adequate, responsive clerical
support is a minimum requirement to support this latter kind
of institutionalization.

In Altona the CSW is not highly institutionalized. There
is no executive director and the chairperson has done little to
procure greater staff support. She explains this lack of effort
by claiming that even in the absence of pressure from the

CSW, elected officials in Altona generally could be relied on to make the right decision when issues came into their domain. Elaborating this point she said: "There are problems, of course, but we have full support anytime, in anything we want to do. The things that are holding women back are really in the private sector. . . I'm not so sure that we could keep an executive director busy . . . . We don't have that much work to be done." In short, the basic mechanism for making policy decisions at the local level does not act against women's interest. CSW attention is required more at the implementation stage; hence the watchdog or investigative role emerged as a high priority in Altona.

Watchdogging/Investigation

The watchdog/investigative activity was ranked among the top three goal/activity areas by three commissions: Marysville County, St. George County, and Altona. For these commissions, watchdogging as an activity implies a conviction that they can stir up matters in the community and yet survive the uproar. The standard fare is to publicize the behavior of powerful institutions and interests. In one community this activity translated into probing for violations of Occupational Safety and Health Administration (OSHA) standards by gathering data on the level of harmful chemicals in breast milk of women working in an electronics plant. In another it meant reviewing recent personnel decisions as a means of challenging the hiring practice of police and fire departments. In a third, it led to launching a campaign against the sexist advertising of local car dealers. What is shared by all three of these commissions and absent in Dodge County and Onega is the experience of positive governmental response to an active watchdogging role. Since watchdogging inevitably leads to opposition from those who are exposed, this activity area generates the most heat. Only commissions with some assurance of backup from their appointing officials will risk this type of engagement.

Convener/Catalyst

The convener/catalyst goal area ranks among the top three activity areas in two CSWs, Onega and Dodge, and is tied with needs assessment for third place in Altona. The simple fact of minimal staff support strongly fosters assigning a high priority to this type of activity in Altona. One commissioner reported: "We have to act as a catalyst. That's about all we can do!"

But in Onega and Dodge community background factors emerge as still more significant variables. The women's movement is not highly institutionalized in either of these communities. Commissioners and activists alike see substantial community opposition to the media image of "women's liberation." Both of these commissions report that opponents from the community have attended commission meetings in order to gather evidence to justify eliminating the CSW, resulting in periods of great harassment. While in both communities feminist activists have existed for some time, the general tenor of neither community is supportive of feminist activism.

Based on this analysis one might conclude that convener/catalyst activity becomes more important when the CSW is the only visible outlet for the expression of women's policy concerns. In other words when the structure of support for women's issues generally is not well developed. Individual activists who want to see a coalition formed on a specific issue, like rape awareness or battered wives, will go to the CSW and ask it to function as the convener. While this involvement has evolved in one instance into actually running a program - on rape awareness - for a period of time, the model in the minds of the staff and members of these commissions is to avoid making such activities permanent CSW programs. Their hope is to provide instead the initial organizational setting for the program development, coupled with the impetus to spin the program off into the community.

Needs Assessment

Ad hoc Commissions on the Status of Women, charged primarily with needs assessment, typically precede the establishment of permanent CSWs; each commission studied here conformed to this pattern. The "needs" demonstrated by this initial group justify the establishment of a commission and most commissions carry on for a couple of years on the basis of this first needs assessment before coming to a period of reassessment. When reassessment comes it often yields a call for a new needs assessment, either general or, more frequently, targeted, or a call for reorganization - collapsing committees, creating new committees, etc.

In Altona the ranking of needs assessment in the top three activity areas appears tied to the fact that the commission is now going through that cyclical reevaluation. An Altona commission member reported about the first needs assessment: "That was certainly of top importance in the beginning. Then it became less important because we had to balance it by what we could do." This balancing appears to involve a second, albeit much more limited, commitment to needs assessment activity. Typically the commission accomplishes this second effort less formally under the direction of small committees.

Expansion of Political Participation and
Direct Supporting Services

Two activity areas ranked as low priority across all CSWs studied are expanding political participation of women and providing direct support services. The low importance assigned to expansion of political participation of women is especially interesting in light of the importance assigned to increased participation in all of the enabling documents. Some documents present this objective in a very general mandate: "To encourage involvement of women in matters pertaining to community progress." In others it appears as a specific program goal: "To provide . . . information concerning qualified women . . . to be submitted to the Governor, Mayor, and to all governmental bodies for appointments to boards, commissions and any governmental vacancies. . . ." Uniformly, it constitutes an early priority.

In part, the fact that a new objective situation has relieved some of the early pressure explains this lower priority. The CSWs have, for example, already served as political springboards for a number of women, with a few of the commissions having had two and three commissioners running for electoral office at a time. Many commissioners believe that they have made a sufficient contribution in this area. Additionally, the Women's Political Caucus seems to be filling gaps which still exist in terms of opportunities for women to run for public office. Thus commissioners often respond to the political participation question by saying, "It's really being done elsewhere," usually naming the Women's Political Caucus specifically as the group now responsible in that area. In most cases the interaction of these two factors has deemphasized the role of the commission in expanding political participation of women, so that this goal-activity area is not likely to reemerge as a major element in the role definition of these local Commissions on the Status of Women.

However, the provision of direct support services is another matter. While this activity area ranks low everywhere, even when the financial commitment to it is high, as in Marysville County, there appears to be a growing interest on the part of the staff in the possibility of providing greater direct support services. The interest for the commission as a whole, however, is strongly disavowed by commission members, many of whom seem well aware of the impact this emphasis might have on the balance of power between staff and citizen commissioners. Direct support services require an enlarged staff to meet programmatic commitments. Commission members perceive quite correctly that the growth of staff means increased autonomy for the executive director - an implication frowned on by most citizen commissioners.

In discussing the activities of commissions thus far the analysis has focused on the contrasting priorities assigned goal-activity areas. Examining the degree of specialization adds another dimension to this analysis. To what extent do these commissions specialize in particular goal-activity areas, and what appears to explain the variation? Deleting direct support services from analysis, because of the difficulty of interpreting responses in light of the staff-CSW member divergence of opinion and its low-priority assignment across the board, the commissions can be grouped by specialization of goal activity. To be considered highly specialized a commission must show a difference of more than one point between the high- and low-importance scores. This analysis assumes that when a commission's mean importance scores across activity areas are close together (i.e., the difference is under 1 point) the commission has not effectively implemented specialization.

The most striking characteristic of the two commissions exhibiting a marked specialization, St. George and Marysville, is that they enjoy a substantially higher level of funding than the other three commissions, thus permitting larger and definitely more professional staffs. The executive directors in these communities, much to the dismay of some commissioners, play a strong leadership role. Hypothetically a more professional administrator in the lead means greater weight behind setting up goals and priorities, resulting in a more intense commitment to a few goal activities. This set of relationships between budget, professionalization of staff and conscious goal setting holds at least a plausible explanation for the distinction between the variation in specialization found.

Summarizing the relationship between the goal activities commissions stress and their context characteristics six such context characteristics appear salient. The organizational factors of size (staff size and membership size), commission age and formal goals, the community setting variable of support structure, and finally the responsiveness of the appointing officials all played a role in shaping the goal activity priorities. However, when looking at the relationship between the degree of specialization in commission goal activities and context characteristics two additional factors seemingly illuminate differences across commissions. Level of funding coupled with the distribution of power between the citizen commissioners and the staff appear related to the degree of specialization commissions exhibit.

SHAPING THE COMMISSION ISSUE AGENDA

Questions about how issues are defined and how they gain placement on a political agenda have generated considerable scholarly debate in recent years.(12)   This study simplifies the query to some extent by acknowledging the existence of a relatively comprehensive delineation of relevant issues drawn from the National Women's Agenda.   The earlier overview of CSWs issue agenda reported a degree of consensus across the five commissions on a few of the very high and very low priority issues.   One by-product of that overview was to dispel the notion that Commissions on the Status of Women intentionally gear their activities to comfortable middle-class women; survival issues, in a very basic sense, dominated the top spots on the summary agenda.

But what of the variation that does occur across communities on the issue agenda?   Is it systematic?   Can it be reasonably explained in terms of the contextual variables named in table 3.3?   Answering these questions requires careful examination of issues where variation does occur.   This discussion focuses on those cases where clear relationships between characteristics and issue priorities are reinforced by supplementary information provided by respondents in the communities.   Table 3.5 presents the prioritized issue agenda for each commission.

Child Care

Child care is a matter of some concern to all CSWs studied, ranking as one of the top-priority issues in the overview discussion presented above.   Many commissioners express this issue concern as fundamental to all others.   One commissioner reported, "If women don't have proper care for their children, they can't do anything else."   Virtually all commission members see child care as a women's issue and think of the issue in a fairly programmatic sense, as number of centers, hours open, space constraints, etc.

The distinction among commissions on the child care issue occurs in terms of the degree of importance assigned by the leadership to the issue.   Three commissions rate child care as the first- or second-priority issue; two commissions fail to include it in the top seven issues.   The distinguishing feature of these latter two commissions is that they operate in communities where strong child care coalitions have emerged.   The commissions in both cases participate, through a liaison person, with the coalition; but the coalition itself is clearly autonomous.   Local officials defer to the coalition as the repository of citizen expertise on child care questions.

Table 3.5. Rank Ordering on Importance of Issue:
All Commissions

Issues	Commissions				
	Marysville	Onega	Dodge	Altona	St. George
Education/training	2	4.5	3	16	6
Employment	3	8	11.5	5	2
Child care	10	2.5	2	2	14
Health care	17	16	15.5	1	11
Political participation	14.5	10	7.5	11	17
Credit	4	6	10	13.5	9.5
Insurance	12	4.5	13	15	18
Tax law	14.5	17	17	19.5	19
Housing	17.5	11.5	15.5	18	6
Rape	1	2.5	9	7	3.5
ERA	7	7	1	9.5	15
Family planning	17	19	18	3.5	16
Female offenders	12	14.5	6	19.5	6
Abortion	19.5	18	19	6	8
Sexual preference	19.5	20	20	17	20
Battered women	7	1	7.5	3.5	9.5
Psychology of women	7	14.5	14	13.5	12.5
Media	9	11.5	11.5	9.5	1
Ethnic-minority issues	12	13	5	8	3.5
Legal, marriage/family	5	9	4	12	12.5

One could, of course, speculate as to why coalitions outside of the CSWs emerged in these two communities. Was there a vacuum left by the CSW in the child care area which another citizen group was bound to fill? There is reason to suspect this may be the case, and that this vacuum may be linked to the relative strength of the staff versus the citizen commissioners. In St. George and Marysville, where the staff is strong, child care rates substantially lower on the agenda (14 and 10, respectively) than it does in Altona, Onega and Dodge, where the staff is markedly weaker. The St. George executive director provided the key to understanding this difference between staff and commissioner perspective when she explained that because child care needs by their nature call for heavy programmatic response, this issue demands greater attention than any executive director can legitimately give without jeopardizing objectives in a wider range of issue areas. (While the St. George commission staff did submit a proposal for county child care funding, the commitment has been minimal in light of the fact that child care ranked as top priority in the needs assessment. When the proposal was not funded, the idea was dropped.) Commissions with weaker executive directors, on the other hand, may never be in the position to make that kind of balancing choice. In Altona, where child care ranks second on the agenda, decision making rests entirely with the citizen group; the part-time staff sees its role as primarily clerical. In Onega and Dodge, where child care rates 2.5 and 2, respectively, the staff perceives even its limited activism as the lesser of two evils. Executive directors in both communities report taking the initiative where necessary to fill gaps, but express a preference, as one director noted, for "working for competent, active, and thorough commissioners where possible."

Thus it may be that where the staff is dominant, child care will have a lower priority, allowing outside coalitions to emerge; where the commissioners dominate, child care will receive high priority, irrespective of its implications for the entire commission program. In both Onega and Dodge, child care rose to such prominence as a result of the intense interest of a single commission member who championed the child care cause within the commission - a cause which, as the St. George executive director would predict, has virtually dominated both commissions for extended periods of time.

In sum, the distribution of commissioner/staff control over decisions interacts with the inclination to activism on the part of the citizen commissioners on substantive issues to produce the different sets of priorities apparent on the child care issue.

Employment

Many commissioners perceive action in the area of employment, as in the area of child care, as fundamental to improvement in women's life chances. Yet only three of the five commissions rated employment as one of the top five issues. Careful examination of the two commissions rating employment lower reinforces the point introduced earlier on the importance of leadership quality in commissioner-dominant commissions, especially in the light of their goal-setting processes.

One commission chairperson explained the agenda setting process in commissioner-dominant commissions this way: "Often goals are determined by the individuals who we have as members of our commission, and their own personal goals: how much time they're willing to commit to it, how much prior knowledge they already had in certain given areas." Thus, in such a commission if a person with a little time, energy, or commitment is put in charge of an important committee, the issue concerns of that committee will soon decline in real importance for the CSW. The two commissions that rate employment of lesser importance are commissioner-dominant commissions. The commissioners themselves explain in each case the relatively low importance assigned to employment in terms of employment committee leadership. "That [employment] should be very important to the commission, but I'm afraid it isn't," or "The Employment Committee is just not a strong committee," commissioners report apologetically.

The failure to recognize the crucial role played by committee chairpersons in citizen-based commissions can lead a CSW to follow an irrational selection strategy. For example, one CSW chairperson arranged for the appointment of the director of the chamber of commerce to the commission, making him the chairperson of the employment committee. A disillusioned commissioner on that commission described the employment chairperson's attitude as hostile to affirmative action, but she explained that the commission leadership had supported reappointing him because, ". . . they believed that by wooing him into activity . . . [the Commission] might get [support]." All however generally acknowledge that, "So far support has not come." In a citizen-based CSW, an unwise committee appointment in an important area can reorient commission priorities in a way that satisfies no one.

Self-Assertiveness/Psychology of Women

In only one commission did the issue of self-assertiveness/psychology of women emerge as a relatively high-priority issue. Conventional wisdom would suggest that a certain level of community affluence inevitably correlates with salience of such postsurvival issues.(13)   However, in comparing the issue priorities of the five communities studied here affluence appears as a necessary but not sufficient cause.   Marysville County where this issue concern ranked seventh is indeed an affluent county, but so is St. George County where the issue ranks substantially lower (12.5) on the issue priority list.

In Marysville the executive director answered a question about which need areas were most pressing for women in the county by saying: "The laws have been passed, and a lot of awareness has been raised; and as a result a lot of women are changing their lives.   And, also are finding themselves caught in situations that are frightening. . . ."   To the same question a commission member responded,

> I think white, middle class women are suffer-
> ing in this country from acute benign neglect.   They
> think, "My husband's earning an income; I don't
> really have to work."   There's no thought about
> having a separate identity of who you are, not being
> somebody's wife or mother or where you live, the
> inhabitant of a particular dwelling.   My personal
> feeling is that the solution is not for every woman to
> have a job, but to have the option and to know,
> really know, what the options are and what the
> stumbling blocks are.

Another commissioner asserted simply: [that] . . . the mental health thing and all that encompasses is the most pressing." Still another commissioner from Marysville chided the national women's movement for neglecting the psychic needs of women: "I think we need not to neglect. . . the emotionally. . . needy woman, whether she needs money or not."

The probable source of the relatively high priority assigned in Marysville County is interorganizational setting of this CSW.   In addition to a Commission on the Status of Women the county runs a women's center.   While organizationally distinct, the executive director of the CSW also serves as head of the women's center staff.   A major commitment of the center is to provide psychological support services to community women.   While the executive director is formally occupying two distinct roles, her identification with the issue priorities of the center inevitably shade her view of proper CSW priorities. Given that the staff dominates on the Marysville commission the high priority the executive director gives to psychological support concerns carries over into a surprisingly high priority attached to this issue by the commission overall.

The Marysville commission doesn't see these psychological support issues as entirely divorced from the classic bread-and-butter issues.   The executive director, who perceives the linkage most clearly, argues: "The psychology of women issue

. . . is really tied into the economics issue . . . because
. . . establishing human relationships is part of and dependent upon establishing a viable person who functions as a
separate individual." Still the psychological support issue
itself holds an unusually high place on the CSW agenda, a
ranking seemingly gained by virtue of the organizational
setting in which the CSW operates.

Credit and Insurance

Credit and insurance are not issues that lend themselves to
action by citizen commissions. To act effectively at the
institutional level in this area requires a substantial expertise.
Thus, it is somewhat surprising to see the issue of credit in
Marysville County and insurance in Onega ranked in the top
five issues for the commissions as a whole.

The distinguishing feature in these two cases is the
appointment to the commission of a professional activist in each
of these areas. This is not to say merely the appointment of a
banker or an insurance broker to a CSW will automatically
result in the emergence of credit and/or insurance as a
high-priority issue. But it is to suggest that the appointment
of a professional who is also an activist for women's rights in
her professional areas, does tend to produce the observed
impact on CSW priorities. This membership variable alone
appears to explain the variation found in this issue.

Abortion

As table 3.2 indicates, abortion as an issue in the years
1974-77 took a back seat to the more pressing "survival"
concerns of women. Part of this is explained by the fact that
the Supreme Court had resolved the basic issue of legal access
to abortion in the 1973 decisions, and had not yet imposed the
restriction on the access for poor women that was to come in
the Beal versus Doe and Maher versus Roe decisions of June
1977. Stll we know from nationwide studies conducted in the
interim years that abortion continued to remain a problem, not
in terms of "legal right" questions, but rather in terms of
practical access.(14)

On the importance assigned to the abortion issue, the five
commissions studied form two types of responses. Three
commissions, Onega, Dodge, and Marysville, rank abortion as
among the three least significant issues, while Altona and St.
George place it among the top ten issues of concern. Predictably organizational and resource characteristics have little
to do with this variation. More surprising is the apparent
lack of relationship between the percent Catholics serving on

the commission and the priority ranking. Rather the principal distinguishing characteristic appears to be governmental responsiveness or more specifically anticipated governmental response to action.

In each of those three commissions ranking abortion extremely low, the chief executive officer of the jurisdiction is publicly opposed to the "pro-choice" position on abortion and enjoys the political support of right-to-life groups. Neither condition holds true in the two commissions ranking abortion in the top ten issues. Commission members in each of the three "low-abortion" commissions explained to me their mayor's position, and named it as part of the rationale for the low ranking. Interviews with these mayors confirmed the accuracy of the commissioners' perception. The cost of taking a pro-choice stand, in face of strong opposition from these powerful men, is more than the CSW chooses to bear. The Onega abortion controversy illustrates this point.

In Onega the abortion issue surfaced without the commission taking the initiative. A local reporter "discovered" in the city employee insurance program a provision for covering both hospital costs for abortions and maternity benefits for unmarried employees. As a right-to-life supporter, he articulated his shock and dismay at this discovery in a lead editorial in the city's major newspaper. This revelation brought immediate proclamations from the mayor and certain council members of their opposition to abortion, and they vowed to make such coverage the topic of the next council session. The mayor claimed ignorance of the abortion provision, which had in fact been part of the insurance packet since 1966. He admitted being aware of the new maternity benefits for unmarried women on the city payroll but claimed to oppose it, explaining: "I was told by the Personnel Department that we would be discriminating against women if the provision wasn't included . . . and . . . that if someone took us to court over it, we would lose."

The first topic on the next council meeting's agenda was an ordinance that would eliminate abortion coverage and maternity coverage for unmarried women. The council indicated unanimously that it wanted abortion coverage removed, though it was split on the pregnancy coverage for unmarried women. An attorney active in the right-to-life organization had assisted the council in drawing up the new ordinance; and the antiabortionists were putting a great deal of pressure on the mayor, who was then running for the United States Senate. A date for the hearing was set, and the bill placed the whole Onega antiabortion movement on the one side, and the Commission on the Status of Women on the other. During seemingly endless hours of testimony the executive director of the CSW tried to make the case that, while the CSW had never taken a position on the issue of abortion, the commission is

vitally concerned about comprehensive insurance coverage for
female city employees. The effort to deflect the hostility by
framing the issue in terms of "insurance" failed. Tempers
flared, as exemplified by the testimony of one right-to-life
activist who referred to the executive director and other
female city employees as "city hall chippies." The CSW lost
the battle; the mayor won the Senate seat; and the matter of
abortion is not likely to be raised by the Commission on the
Status of Women again. By arguing, albeit indirectly, for the
right to choose, the CSW brought out all of those in the community who wished to see the commission eliminated. During
the time of this debate representatives from right-to-life
organizations monitored the CSW meetings. The very existence
of the CSW appeared temporarily threatened. To at least one
commission member the lesson was clear: from now on "we will
completely avoid that issue."

It is useful to note that the distinction between commissions ranking abortion at the bottom of the agenda and those
who rank it higher is not simply based on the cohesiveness of
the commissioners on the issue. The commissioners as a group
are in some disagreement in four of the five commissions. Nor
does the experience of having been through a confrontation
with the right-to-life group in itself lead to the very low
priority. The case of St. George County illustrates this latter
point.

The St. George commission voted to support the Supreme
Court decision in 1973 (Roe versus Wade/Doe versus Bolton)
and attempted to secure county council endorsement for that
decision. During the course of events the CSW was directed
by the council to hold hearings allowing the right-to-life
groups an opportunity to present their side. The CSW staff
and members of the executive board received numerous
threatening and abusive phone calls and endured other forms
of personal harassment shortly before and after the hearings.
It all ended in the local council voting to endorse the initial
stand taken by the commission. While the issue of abortion
has not been raised again by the commission as a top-priority
issue, the sense remains that abortion is an area of legitimate
CSW concern. The general responsiveness of the council members to the commission action on abortion in this case seems to
have fostered a belief that the commission could take a pro-
choice stand in the future without severe threat to survival.
That conviction is clearly absent from the three commissions
rating abortion at the bottom of their priority list.

Legal Rights in Marriage and Family

Legal rights in marriage and family ranks among the top
five issues in two communities, Marysville and Dodge. One

experience shared by these CSWs is distinct success in a major legislative battle in this area. In Dodge County the commission got behind an effort to reform state family law that was led by one of their own members, who also served on the state Commission on the Status of Women. In Marysville County the legislative action at the state level was in the area of sexual assault with special emphasis on the intrafamily assault. In each case the CSW committed substantial resources to the endeavor, and that resource commitment helped to bring about the desired legislative action.

This kind of experience, for a period of time after the victory at least, appears to result in sustaining a high level of interest in doing "more of the same." Commissioners reported, in light of these victories, that this area seemed to be one in which they could be effective. Again governmental responsiveness appears to be the key, albeit in a slightly different form than demonstrated in the abortion issue. In the abortion case governmental responsiveness might translate into a vote in support of a commission position on an issue, but its most significant meaning is as a vote of confidence in the commission itself. But in these domestic legal rights cases governmental responsiveness refers to positive governmental action on an issue. The victory is in producing the desired action.

Ethnic/Minority

Ethnic/minority is considered as a separate issue area in recognition of the fact that ethnic and minority women may be doubly disadvantaged and thus present intensified needs across a number of issues. It placed among the top five issues in two of the communities, though well-organized ethnic or minority groups exist in three communities studied. In the two commissions, Dodge and St. George, where ethnic/minority scores highest as an issue, there are formally designated ethnic/minority committees within the commission. The source of this formal designation appears to be the narrowness of support for the CSW in the ethnic or minority communities. In both of the cases where ethnic/minority issues rank high, women representing ethnic/minority groups on the commission continue to harbor great suspicion about the intentions of their fellow commission members. Both of these commissions have experienced serious internal struggles over the extent to which CSW action truely represents ethnic/minority interests. In both cases the emphasis is on hispanic ethnic groups and there is a strong feeling that the CSW as a whole has no motivation to respond to a non-Anglo community.

In Altona where ethnic/minority issues rate a lower score on the agenda, the CSW membership does include very active representatives of ethnic communities. In fact it has always had as an objective equal representation for anglos, latins and blacks. Thus ethnics on the Altona CSW respond to the ethnic/minority issue question by saying: "We don't break it down that way." It appears that here the ethnic/minority members are much more fully integrated into the decision-making structure of the commission and hence bring an "ethnic" perspective to all issues on which the CSW acts. Because one of the objectives of the commission there has been to insure this integration, the relationship between the CSW and the ethnic/minority community is such that representation per se is not an issue. In other words it appears that the structure of support for the commission and the appointment guidelines of the CSW interact to produce the differences in priority given this issue by Altona as opposed to Dodge and St. George.

Sexual Preference

Sexual preference ranks as the issue of least importance for four of the five commissions and seventeenth out of twenty issues for the fifth commission. Perhaps the most interesting aspect of this ranking is the uniformity across commissions. This uniform response is somewhat surprising for it suggests that, notwithstanding variation in structural arrangements, in the general responsiveness of local governments, and, most especially, in this extent to which lesbian interests are mobilized in the community, CSW response will remain unchanged.

Typically the CSW leadership and staff answer questions on the importance of the sexual preference issue by saying simply "that is not one of our issues." The rationale for "why not" varies. One of four explanations is given: 1) lesbians are not sufficiently organized for commissions to respond to their needs, 2) sexual preference doesn't relate to women only, 3) dealing with lesbianism would destroy the commission, or 4) it is a civil rights issue, properly the concern of the human relations commission.

Marysville County falls into the first category. The commissioners seem genuinely unaware of organized lesbian interests. They speculate that lesbians tend not to live in Marysville County; or if they do, they must channel their political activities through organizations in neighboring cities.

Dodge County is less able to dismiss the lesbian issue on the "no constituency" grounds. The issue had fractured the NOW organization in that community, and a gay rights ordinance had been a major point of political controversy. Nevertheless the commission responded to a request for support from the gay community by stating, in the words of the executive director: "We have never taken a position on anything that doesn't strictly apply to women alone."

The Onega CSW also faced a challenge from organized lesbian interests, who, through a CSW member, requested first that a workshop co-sponsored by NOW and the CSW focus on the issue of lesbianism, and second, that the CSW ask the mayor to establish a task force on lesbians in the community. The chairperson of the CSW denied both requests, thus engendering great disappointment and anger in the lesbian community. Dealing directly with the practical political problems involved, the chairperson stressed the significance of the fact that the mayor was at that time running for the United States Senate. The executive director, however, spoke to the issue more generally, justifying the shunning of sexual preference as an issue because, "we are politically oriented. It would be death for us."

The CSW in the two communities where lesbians are most fully mobilized gave a fourth rationale for CSW decisions to relegate the sexual preference question to the bottom of the list. In both communities certain lesbian organizations are well known to CSW members. When asked about the salience of sexual preference as an issue the CSW members and staff respond that sexual preference is a civil rights issue, and is thus under the charge of the human relations commission, not the CSW. It is not, as such, a women's rights issue. A staff member in one of the communities explains the arrangement in this way: "Lesbian women seem to divide their political life between women's groups and gay groups and haven't come to us as part of those gay groups." The rationale for the low priority assigned to sexual preference varies, but consensus exists on one point across all commissions: dissociation from lesbianism is vital.

Summarizing the relationship between issue concerns commissions stress and the context in which they operate, eight such contextual factors emerge as salient. Two of these factors, the responsiveness of appointing officials and the structure of support for women's issues in the community, play a role in shaping the issue agenda as well as the goal-activity priorities of the commissions discussed above. The remaining six factors appear associated solely with positioning of issues on the commission agenda. Membership characteristics (occupation and substantive interest of commissioners), organizational characteristics (appointment procedures for commission members and committee chairpersons and distribution of staff/commissioner control) and community characteristics (sources and breadth of CSW support) seemingly contribute to shaping the issue agenda in these five communities.

Table 3.6 presents an overview of the relationships between certain characteristics of the context in which these five commissions function and commission judgments regarding the priority of both goal activities and issues. One major objective of this chapter was simply to examine in-depth the

Table 3.6. Context Characteristics and Goal-Activity/Issue Priorities: A Summary of Apparent Relationships

	Membership		Organizational								Community Background		Governmental Responsiveness
Goal Activities	Occupation	Substantive Interest	Size of CSW	Inter-Organizational Setting	Size of Staff	Appointment of CSW	Distribution of Citizen/Staff Control	Appointment of Committee Leadership	CSW Age	CSW Formal Goals	Breadth of Support	Structure of Support	Responsiveness of Decision-Making/Appointed Officials
Public education										*			
Direct influence					*								*
Watchdog investigative													*
Convener/catalyst			*								*	*	
Needs assessment									*				
Issues													
Child care		*					*						
Employment								*					
Self-assertiveness/psychology of women				*			*						
Credit/insurance	*	*											
Abortion													*
Legal rights													*
Ethnic/minority						*					*		
Sexual preference													

62

goal activities of commissions and their issue agenda. But an equally important aim was to provide an inductively sound basis for developing hypotheses about the contextual correlates of the activity and issue choices commissions make. Presented in this setting table 3.6 stands both as a framework for self-study accessible to local Commissions on the Status of Women and as a preliminary research agenda for future studies of the forces shaping such organizational choices.

4 Commissions and Community Activists: Performance as Agenda Building

The whole matter of how issues get on the political agenda of local governing bodies has attracted considerable attention in recent years. A significant body of scholarship focuses on agenda building as an area of inquiry capable of providing answers to the knotty problem of reconciling classical democratic theory with the empirical reality of a nonactivist citizenry.(1) While the negative critics of the Commissions on the Status of Women may see the establishment of a CSW as the substitution of a symbolic reward - a kind of placebo - for genuine action on issues of concern to community women, other observers have argued that CSWs have legitimized the public airing of previously suppressed issues vital to women.(2) This chapter explores the role played by high-performing commissions in the area of agenda building.

Recent political science literature elaborates the raison d'etre for an agenda-building focus. Cobb and Elder tell us that "the range of issues and decision alternatives that will be considered by a polity is restricted." This restriction arises from two sources. The first is a systems imperative, and is predicated on the fact that the processing and attention capabilities of any human organization are necessarily limited. The second source of restriction arises from the fact that "all forms of political organization have a bias in favor of the exploitation of some kinds of conflict and the suppression of others because organization is the mobilization of bias. Some issues are organized into politics while others are organized out."(3)

The key questions, from the perspective of a newly mobilized interest, are: Who participates in this agenda-building process and how does one gain access to the political agenda? Once interests in the community at large have defined certain matters as salient, how do those matters translate into

issues?   Cobb and Elder frame this question in terms of the
gap between the systemic agenda, i.e., "a general set of
political controversies that will be viewed at any point in time
as falling within the range of legitimate concerns meriting the
attention of the polity," and the institutional agenda, i.e., "a
set of concrete, specific items scheduled for active and serious
consideration by a particular institutional decision-making
body."(4)
     Partisans of CSWs see them as bodies designed to bridge
the gap between the systemic and institutional definitions of
the women's agenda.   Simply by taking up issues and assigning them high priority for CSW action, commissions place
issues on the institutional agenda for their local jurisdictions.
To what extent do commissions adopt issues championed by
women's groups in the community and make those issues a
focus of concern and interest within the political system?
Admittedly, framing the question in this way does little to
illuminate the impact commissions make on certain issues.
Simply placing an issue on an institutional agenda does not
guarantee a satisfactory resolution.   Nonetheless placement is
obviously a prerequisite.   From that perspective the role
played by a CSW in articulating the important issues for women
in the community becomes critical.
     Agenda building accordingly emerges as one of the three
operational criterion for exploring performance.   Whereas
chapters 2 and 3 considered performance simply in terms of
organizational activity – what commissions do – analysis now
takes a more evaluative turn in considering the purposes or
intent of commissions.   Building women's issues into the
institutional agenda is a major intent of Commissions on the
Status of Women.   To determine the extent to which the five
high-performing commissions studied actually bridged the gap
between the systemic and institutional forms of the women's
agenda in each community, I looked at the congruence between
the issue agenda of women's organization activists and the
commission agenda.

ISSUES AND THE RESPECTIVE AGENDA

An issue emerges when there is conflict between groups over
substantive or procedural matters relating to the distribution
of that which is valued in a polity.(5) Women's policy issues,
more specifically, arise where there is conflict between groups
over some aspect of public policy which directly impacts on
women by shaping their life chances either covertly or
overtly.(6)   At the local level, the women's agenda consists of
those issues salient to women in a particular community.

The last chapter told much of the story on the commission agenda in the communities studied. There the commission, or "institutional" agenda was empirically represented in a straight-forward fashion using mean responses of commission leadership to a question requiring the assignment of importance scores to 20 women's policy issues. In this chapter we are concerned with the extent to which the CSW is representing, on the institutional agenda, those issue concerns and priorities operating in the broader community of women. Assessing the performance of the commissions in this sphere involves first identifying those groups representing actual women's interests in the community and second, ascertaining the issue agenda of those groups.

In identifying the relevant "interest" organizations whose priorities reflect the systemic women's agenda, preliminary conceptual problems revolve around the need to distinguish among interest groups, social movements, and movement organizations. The literature defines an interest group as "an organized social aggregation which seeks political goals it is incapable of providing for itself."(7) It is to be distinguished from a social movement in which interest groups or pressure groups may take part, but which itself represents "a generalized progression of public opinion" untied to a specific organization.(8)

While the "women's movement" is a term often used in the discussion of activities of organized women's interest groups, Jo Freeman has correctly pointed out the distinction between the women's movement and organized activist groups.(9) Within the women's movement there are organizations, such as the National Organization for Women, which owe their existence to the movement in a very direct sense. But in addition to these organizations, which are part of the very texture of the new feminism, there are also other kinds of voluntary organizations that hold the advancement of women's interests as a primary objective. In local politics especially, these organizations become part of the pressure system advancing movement objectives. At the nominal level, then, any organization could qualify as a women's activist organization if it were visibly change oriented,(10) and if the advocated change aimed to advance women's movement values. To qualify as a women's activist group, the organization would not have to be an ideologically feminist group.

Determining the systemic women's agenda in a particular community requires looking at the women's agenda of the major women's activist organizations. Thus the first empirical task is to identify this set of organizations for each community. This research took a largely reputational tack, utilizing the League of Women Voters and National Organization for Women as anchor points.

The initial design called for interviewing the National Organization for Women and League of Women Voters chairpersons in each community. It was taken for granted that the League of Women Voters, because of its historical connection with the first women's movement, its documented liberal bias, but most especially because of its recent national emphasis on ERA ratification, would emerge in every community as one of the most visible and influential women's activist organizations. It was also assumed that the prototypical women's movement organization, National Organization for Women, though less well organized at the local level, would be a key actor in formulating the feminist component of the systemic agenda. These preliminary judgments about the local organizational map generally proved sound, with the single exception that NOW did not function in one community. The Women's Political Caucus (WPC) had emerged in that community to represent the feminist viewpoint locally.

The choice of the League of Women Voters and National Organization for Women (and the Women's Political Caucus in one case) drew additional support from responses to a question asking commission leadership and staff to name the most visible and/or effective women's activist groups in the community. This question elicited, in addition to the LWV, NOW, and WPC, designation of a number of other groups. After the commissioner and staff interviews I then asked the LWV and NOW (or WPC) chair the same question, thus providing a rounded perspective on the four or five organizations that were perceived to fit best the "women's activist group" designation in each community. Other groups mentioned included Business and Professional Women, AAUW, women's centers, welfare organizations, the Junior League, ethnic women's organizations, black sororities, lesbian organizations, collectives for third world women, peer counseling collectives and a women employee's association. Predictably the set of four or five groups varied across communities, with the LWV and NOW (with the exception noted) remaining constant.

Extensive interviews of the formal leaders of these organizations revealed the women's systemic agenda in each community. During the course of each interview activists assessed the importance (scale 1 to 5) of the 20 major women's policy issues introduced in chapter 3. This data resulted in a measure of community activist priorities, which provided a basis for comparing the systemic agenda to the institutional agenda articulated by the CSW.

Comparing activist interviews across communities one is struck by the variation in the extent to which community activists articulate an agenda compatible with that of the CSW. Table 4.1 reports in a quantitative form the relationship between the commission and activist issue agenda in the five communities.

Table 4.1.   Degree of Relationship between Rank Ordering
             on Issue Agenda:*   CSW and Activist

Community	Spearman Correlation Coefficient
Altona	0.72
Onega	0.67
St. George County	0.64
Marysville County	0.47
Dodge County	0.18

*N = 20 issues.
Note: Once again, the names of the communities have
been changed to protect the anonymity of persons interviewed.

Clearly these correlations suggest significant differences,
borne out by the interviews, in the extent to which commissions perform this agenda-building role. Looking simply at
the degree of relationship between the activist and commission
agenda in the communities, Altona appears substantially more
effective than Dodge County in performing a conversion role,
i.e., converting issues from the women's activist, or systemic
agenda, to the commission or institutional agenda.
       High-performing commissions report two general modes of
agenda building, one simply responsive and the other involving
initiating rather than responding.   One commission member
described by illustration the responsive mode of agenda
building: "Two women come to you [the commission] and they
say, 'We want to start a women's credit union.' It may not be
at the top of your priorities. It may not even be within your
whole needs assessment.   But if they say, 'We want to do
this,' and we think there is a need, we are certainly going
to do everything we can do to help them."   Help in this
case was in fact limited to providing a list of organizations
which these women should contact and permission to say that
the CSW strongly encouraged the idea of a credit union.
Other activities illustrate the commissions initiating role in
agenda building.   In one commission a few members were
very interested in the health area, particularly with the
restricted access to abortion resulting from the location of the
vacuum aspirator in the surgery department of the local public

hospital. The commission chairperson called a meeting of representatives from each of the social service agencies involved in pregnancy counseling, ranging from Planned Parenthood to the neighborhood health clinics. After trying to ascertain how many abortions had to be referred out of the city, the commission chairperson and a chair of the health committee, with a city council woman and a representative from the mayor's office, visited the hospital administrators and argued for change. Ultimately the vacuum aspirator was placed in the outpatient clinic. Here the CSW not only placed an agenda item, high in salience to the actual community, on the institutional agenda but carried it to successful outcome.

Alternative agenda-building strategies obviously exist. Nevertheless, as table 4.1 indicates, some commissions are high performers and others low performers irrespective of strategy. This phenomenon can be productively explored by juxtaposing the commissions representing the highest and lowest performance on the issue conversion dimension. Table 4.2 reveals the activist agenda, coupled with commission ranking of activist issues for the high and low performers.

Table 4.2. Priority Issues* for Activists,
with CSW Ranking

Dodge County		Altona	
Top Activist Issues	CSW Rank	Top Activist Issues	CSW Rank
ERA	1	Employment	5
Rape	9	Health	1
Family planning	18	Ethnic/minority	8
Sexual preference	20	Rape	7
Female offenders	6	Education and training	16
Battered women	7	Child care	2
Abortion	19	Abortion	6
Ethnic/minority	5	Battered women	3.5

*Eight issues are used for this priority list, rather than the established seven because of the scoring ties in the Dodge County activist group.

As might be expected issue orderings between activists
and CSW members do not mesh perfectly - even in Altona,
where the conversion score is highest. But this table of issue
priorities does reveal that Altona gives high agenda status to
virtually all of the issues most salient to the activist community. The only exception in this case is the matter of
education and training. Dodge County, on the other hand,
where we have found the lowest correlation between activist
and CSW issue agenda, a comparison of the top activist issues
with CSW rankings illuminates the low relationship. Half of
the issues receiving high status on the activist agenda do not
appear among the top eight CSW issues; and, in fact, three of
those highest priority issues from the activist perspective rank
at the very bottom of the women's agenda, as articulated by
the CSW.

What is interesting at first glance about the apparent
variation is its challenge to a number of common preconceptions about the relationship between commission attributes and
performance. An earlier chapter presented five context
characteristics (table 3.3) as factors thought potentially
related to variation in performance. Of those variables neither
organizational characteristics, resources, membership traits,
nor governmental responsiveness appear related in any
systematic way to the capacity of a commission to carry out the
agenda-building function. In other words it makes little
difference whether a commission is legislative or merely
established by executive order, whether it has virtually no
funding or is very well funded, whether government decision
makers act affirmatively on the agenda the CSW institution-
alizes or fail to do so. Rather the key factor related to the
capacity for a CSW to play this "conversion of issues" role is
the community background variable: What was the initial
structure of support for the CSW and did that support
structure endure over time? Descriptions of community
background traits of the high and low performers according to
this agenda conversion criterion illustrate the point.

Dodge County: Origin of the Commission
on the Status of Women

In January of 1971 the board of county commissioners enacted
an ordinance establishing a Commission on the Status of
Women. During the election campaign of 1970 a Dodge County
citizen, who was identified locally and nationally as a feminist
activist, approached all of the candidates for mayor and asked
if they would appoint a mayor's CSW. One candidate agreed
and on the night of his election, the feminist protagonist sent
him a telegram requesting that the CSW establishment proposal
be placed on the agenda of the first council meeting. After

hearings where pro and con forces testified, the council drafted and acted upon an ordinance establishing the commission.

While the original members appointed to the commission were on the whole a distinguished group of citizens, they came to women's issues from at least three distinct perspectives. A few of the original members were women who had opposed the creation of the CSW and avowedly saw their function as negating women's movement objectives. Still others were not ideologically opposed to CSW objectives, but needed to be persuaded that a "problem" existed. A core group of ideologically committed feminists constituted a third element on this charter commission. Distributed across all three groups were a number of women harboring larger political ambitions of their own.

A struggle among the three major groups dominated the early history of the commission, the ultimate impact of which disenchanted those women most closely tied to the women's movement. Rather than requesting reappointment to the commission, or at least sponsoring like-minded women for membership, many feminist activists seem to have forsaken the commission entirely. One former commission member, interviewed because of her leadership role in a major feminist organization, explained: "The activists have moved on . . . [because they] recognized it [the commission] would never be fully effective. . . . They [the commission members] are much less activist now. It's more comfortable that way. It's more difficult to confront. Most women don't want to." Those originally opposed to the establishment of the CSW also became inactive. This left, for the most part, women who required some consciousness raising to understand women's movement issues. Predictably such women do not successfully articulate the women's agenda inside government.

Altona: Origins of the Commission on the Status of Women

In 1974, during the fall elections, the Women's Political Caucus organized a coalition effort among women's groups aimed at selecting women to run for city council. When talking in the spring about what the coalition wanted newly elected women officials to address, it focused on appointment of women to boards and commissions. Accordingly this same group that had worked on the fall elections canvassed openings on boards and commissions in order to secure several female appointments. Stemming from the Women's Political Caucus, but acting now as a separate entity, the group soon felt the need for some structure of its own. One participant in the early meetings reported, "We decided we can't operate this way. We need some kind of formal structure . . . a Commission on the

Status of Women should really be doing this.'" But the group realized that if there were to be a CSW, it would have a broader charge than merely advancing female appointments.

When they reflected on what they wanted a CSW to do, one participant reported that they thought in terms of doing that which the Women's Political Caucus could not easily do. They specifically had in mind what they considered peripherally political functions, such as monitoring health care standards in the obstetrics/gynocology clinic at the local hospital.

Having worked out this rationale on their own, a committee of five women asked the mayor for an ordinance, and he agreed. Because the rationale for a commission had been so thoroughly thought out in advance, and the persons involved at the early stages so well identified, it was natural that these people should receive commission appointments. One member of the original coalition, a Women's Political Caucus activist, had done research on other local commissions, and she assumed the lead. The dissension characterizing the early days of many CSWs never appeared. The commission became the official arm of the women's movement in the city, and every appointee had substantial feminist credentials.

Whether this linkage with the activist community will be maintained is unclear at this point. A comment made by one activist leader introduces some doubt. She reports that in making recommendations for boards and commissions she no longer thinks of the CSW as a high-priority appointment. Instead, she is beginning to put her time into boards and commissions with greater clout in the city. Should such a trend develop, the agenda-building capacity of this CSW would surely suffer. What comes through in this discussion of the community background of the commissions exhibiting the greatest and least capacity for converting issues from the systemic to the institutional agenda, is that variation in this performance is closely related to the sources and structure of commission support at birth and perhaps continuing beyond.

The rationale supporting this thesis is that issue-relevant ties between the commission and the women's activist groups in the community are essential to high performance in the agenda-conversion area and that in order for community activist group leaders and commissions to maintain ties, they must clearly perceive their interdependence. What determines whether or not they will perceive interdependence is not simply the amount of formal overlap in membership, though that may be an indicator; nor is it the self-perceived activism in the women's movement on the part of the commissions that impacts on commission performance. Rather what counts is the extent to which the community activist leaders perceive the commission role clearly in terms of some real task that needs to be done and that an official governmental advisory commission can best do. While hypothetically this legitimacy could be attained by a commission after establishment, in the high- and low-performing commissions used to exemplify the point here, the community background factors seemed to greatly influence the outcome.

It is interesting to note that the self-perception of commission members concerning their own degree of activism in the women's movement bears no relationship to the extent to which that commission actually represents the systemic women's agenda of the larger community. Table 4.3 reports mean activism scores for the commissions with their respective ranking on the agenda-building performance criterion.

Table 4.3. CSW by Activism* of Members and
Agenda-Building Performance Rating

Commission	Mean Activism	Agenda Performance
St. George (N=8)	7.8	3
Dodge County (N=20)	7.7	5
Altona (N=12)	7.6	1
Onega (N=32)	6.9	2
Marysville County (N=13)	6.7	4

*On a 1-to-10 scale.

Put in a broader context, these "sources and structure of support" characteristics touch on the matter of legitimacy. James Q. Wilson, in his work on political organization, stresses that many organizations fail to become invested with the cloak of legitimate authority. Some of these organizations simply dissolve, while others endure only at the price of continuous factionalism or ineffectual blandness.(11) Legitimacy is not, however, a dichotomous variable. Organizations can be more or less invested with the principle of legitimate authority. The analysis of the origins of the two commissions described leads to the conclusion that to close the gap between the systemic and institutional agenda, the activist community must recognize the legitimacy of authority vested in the commission.

ISSUES SHUNNED BY COMMISSIONS

A somewhat different perspective on this agenda-conversion question is achieved through examining the pooled responses of activists and commissioners for all five commissions studied. From an agenda-building perspective one might ask: Are there issues which the commissions as a group are likely to shun? Table 4.4 exhibits those issues for which statistically significant negative relationships existed between responses from activists and CSW members, treating each as a single group.

Table 4.4. Issues Eliciting Significantly Different
Responses from Commissions and Activists:
Difference of Means Test

T Test Scores	Issues		
	Abortion	Sexual Preference	Ethnic Minority
T Value	-2.30	-4.84	-2.29
Significance*	0.02	0.00	0.02

* Probability that T value could occur by chance; 0.02 used as maximum significance score.

Table 4.4 suggests that the placement of these issues on the activist agenda is significantly different from their placement on the CSW agenda. Chapter 3 reviewed the CSW perspective on each of these issues, offering some insight into the rationale commissions used to justify the low placement. That earlier discussion pointed out the difficulty of interpreting the low priority assigned to the ethnic/minority question. Some respondents simply rejected breaking the issue down in that way. Thus, this examination of issues which the commissions shun focuses only on abortion and sexual preference, where the activist perception of "importance" is markedly greater than the CSW view. How do activists interpret this difference?

It is fair to say that for the most part the activists interviewed responded to the commission treatment of these issues with tolerance and some occasionally with understanding. In two of the communities local hospitals refused to perform abortions, obviously constraining access to such operations. Local activists accepted the decision of the commissions to eschew taking a stand on this problem. One League of Women Voters member, though personally alarmed by hospital policy, seemed resigned to the fact that the commission's hands were tied on this matter. She explained that the local Commission on the Status of Women simply could not touch the issue, in part because of the internal dissension it would spark, but more especially because of the antiabortion disposition of the chief executive official to whom the commission reports. Her assessment matched precisely that of the CSW leadership in the community. In a second community a pro-choice activist issued this blanket statement: "The most controversial issues are in the area of reproduction, and they for the most part have been left to NOW." This kind of division of labor seemed to her an acceptable compromise with political reality. Other activists in each of these communities saw the abortion restrictions as a major concern of Planned Parenthood. Since the CSW involvement seemed to add only incrementally to the pro-choice effort, the risk entailed in becoming active on this issue seemed too great.

It is important to remember, however, that these interviews were conducted before the June 1977, Supreme Court decision upholding the right of a state to refuse to spend public funds for elective abortions. If the activists, responding in this understanding way to the CSW issue priorities, saw commission support as essential to getting the abortion access issue onto the local agenda, they might not have been so understanding. In other words, it may have been that since the 1973 Supreme Court decision (Roe versus Wade and Doe versus Bolton) legitimized the abortion debate, the incremental benefit derived from CSW involvement was not worth risking overall CSW effectiveness, in activist eyes. With the pro-choice forces once again on the defensive, since the Beal versus Doe/Maher versus Roe decision (1977), commission treatment of this issue may become less acceptable.

The sexual preference issue is somewhat more complicated than the abortion matter. Here again we have higher agenda status assigned to sexual preference by the activist community than by the CSW. Three commissions studied have confronted sexual preference more or less directly and decided, for the reasons discussed earlier in chapter 3, that sexual preference will not be a commission issue. Unlike the case of abortion access, there is no alternative organization in any of these three communities ready and willing to champion the cause of lesbian rights. Given the possibility, as noted above, of a changed activist assessment of the CSW responsibilities in light of the recent Supreme Court decision on federal support for abortion, one might expect that in the three communities where lesbian rights is an important but unlegitimated issue, the activists most concerned would be intolerant of CSW blinders. Surprisingly this expectation is not borne out. In the case of sexual preference the activists, even leaders in lesbian organizations, seem willing to tolerate the commissions' noninvolvement stance.

One CSW staff member, herself unsure why lesbians have remained so undemanding, recounted a story which encapsulates the lesbian response in the highly activist community of St. George County. It concerned an exchange which took place during a course on women and politics taught by commission staff members at a local university. The course was taught under a special "Political and Social Issue Program," aimed at bringing into the classroom persons on the cutting edge of current issues. The staff members reported:

> The majority of the students in the class were lesbians. I can remember the first class session. One of them brought up the issue of sexual discrimination on the basis of sexual preference, and what a drag it was and how terrible it was and all the problems that she encountered . . . and asked what the commission was doing about it. . . . [The executive director of the CSW] . . . said to her, "It's not our area of jurisdiction, so we can't do anything about it." And this woman, who is really an activist, took that as being fine. "Fine, I understand. That's a good excuse. I'm not going to hassle you over it," and dropped it. And that was it. They never brought it up again.

Intrigued by this apparent complacency on the part of lesbian organizational activists in communities studied, I asked activists (lesbians and nonlesbians) why lesbians did not demand more of the commission. Since the commission might have facilitated the movement of the lesbian rights question to the institutional agenda, why did the lesbian community itself let it "off the hook"? This question elicited two general types of responses. Respondents in two communities explained this phenomenon primarily in terms of the political ideology and the accompanying change strategy of the lesbian community. In three of the communities the explanation resided more in the organizational characteristics of the lesbian community itself.

In both Altona and St. George political ideology emerged in several forms to produce the apparent complacency with the commission position. A proportion of lesbians in each of these communities is separatist in orientation and thus chooses to have as little contact as possible with men. When possible these gay women may act on this choice by moving out of the urban area, establishing an agricultural commune where they can be relatively self-sufficient. If the move to a separatist commune is not possible, these lesbians will make the compromises necessary to survive in an urban area, but not go so far as working with a Commission on the Status of Women. Though the commission itself may be, in some cases, exclusively female, its very nature as a governmental commission implies working with, and depending upon, male governmental officials.

Political ideology also short circuits interaction with the Commission on the Status of Women when the lesbian community is primarily libertarian. Some lesbians, who may or may not be separatists, are politically estranged from government in any form, including the CSW form. As ideological disciples of libertarians such as Ayn Rand, they are primarily concerned with being independent. Thus they resist government intervention in any form whether in their private sex lives or in their business operations. They reject governmental action on their behalf from any source, including Commissions on the Status of Women.

Finally political ideology can play a role in shaping lesbian interaction with the local CSW when that ideology defines the lesbian problem as essentially a gay rights problem. In some communities political interests are highly differentiated, and some lesbians define the sexual preference issue as one of gay rights rather than as women's rights. Such lesbians ally with male gay groups and hence do not see the CSW as a reasonable place to go for a response to their demands.

These three responses, stemming from political ideology, all lead lesbian interests to refrain from pressuring the commissions for space on the policy agenda. A fourth orientation articulated in the activist interviews might be labeled the pragmatic lesbian feminist response - again a kind of political ideology. Here lesbian groups perceive themselves to be relatively well accepted in the "straight" feminist community. They recognize the threat to commission legitimacy, in the eyes of the citizenry, that espousal of lesbian rights could provoke. Believing that reducing the effectiveness of the commission generally - by decreasing its legitimacy through identification with lesbian interests - would be counter to the feminist interest of lesbians, they opt for working with the CSW on feminist issues, while fighting the lesbian battle under a separate banner.

In three communities, Onega, Dodge, and Marysville, political ideology sheds little light on the accommodating character of the lesbian-CSW relationship. In these com-

munities, where lesbian groups are much less visible and less
highly differentiated lesbian tolerance revolves around the
organization of the lesbian community itself.   Three salient
aspects of the lesbian organization emerged from the interviews.   First, many lesbians, even those active in lesbian
organizations, were nonpolitical.   They join lesbian groups
primarily for support and socializing, not viewing the group
as an interest group in any political sense.   Hence they did
not consider the failure of the local Commission on the Status
of Women to take up the matter of lesbian rights as any
particular deprivation.   Second, among those lesbians who did
think in political terms, insufficient group agreement on the
rules of the game militated against any kind of goal information
taking place.   Because a lesbian can be anyone - professional
women, factory worker, or community organizer - agreement on
rules for decision making have yet to be forged.(12)   In one
community this problem of developing a common framework was
all pervasive.   In the middle of a heated debate among a group
of lesbian NOW members on the type of NOW affiliation appropriate for gay women, for example, the matter of the dress
habits of some lesbian women became paramount.   One gay
professional woman complained that she could not bring her
friends to the lesbian group meetings because of the shabby
clothing worn by her sister lesbians.   Needless to say this
comment sparked an intense response from the nonprofessional
women.   Perhaps predictably, the group split apart, with
neither group having sufficient numbers to function effectively
in an advocate role.   In all three of these communities the
matter of lesbian integration into the women's rights movement
virtually incapacitated the NOW organization for a period of
time, with the point of discord being style of activity
acceptable and the degree of NOW commitment required.
Obviously the development of some consensus on basic style
and leadership questions must precede any effort to make
demands on a government body such as a Commission on the
Status of Women.
     Finally, some of those who are active in lesbian groups
remain timid about making demands on a governmental body
when existing state law prohibits their very life-style.   A
certain confidence in one's security in terms of life-style must
support a demand for protection.   Some lesbian group members
simply lack the security necessary to come out of the political
closet.
     In the three communities where these attributes of the
lesbian organization seemed to explain the absence of demands
on the commission, it also appears that such agenda demands,
if articulated, would be difficult for the CSW to meet.   Even if
one were to assume that the total commission, or at least a
substantial majority, could be persuaded of the wisdom of such
a cause - this is unlikely because of strong religious affiliation

of some members - the innate drive for organizational survival would lead the commission decision makers to steer away from such action. For some time organizational theorists have been telling us that whatever else organizations do, they seek to survive.(13)   There is little to suggest that Commissions on the Status of Women would be the exception to this rule, or that they could embrace this issue and survive.

To sum up this study's findings on the agenda-building capacity of Commissions on the Status of Women, one must note the difference in commission capacity to perform this role. Those commissions with an ability to work out an ongoing and vital relationship with organizational activists in the community are most successful in agenda building.   Activists must see the commission as a prime issue forum.   However certain issues are never placed on the institutional agenda, irrespective of their status on the systemic agenda.   Abortion and sexual pref- erence issues illustrate that when this bifurcation of CSW and the activist community occurs, the activists seem to tolerate and generally understand the constraints imposed on CSW agenda building.   While in the case of both abortion and sexual preference there is opposition to CSW sponsorship coming from CSW members, outside activists tend to put the blame on constraints external to the CSW itself.

5 Commissions and Their Audiences: Performance as Effectiveness

The "performance" concept implies at least three criteria for assessing Commissions on the Status of Women. Earlier chapters focused on performance both as capacity to influence future events, and as facility in agenda building. This chapter considers performance in terms of commission effectiveness or impact - the most commonly held criterion. Yet, definitions of effectiveness in this context are as diverse as the CSW audiences.

Commission audience simply refers to a group in the community that, by position or interest, brings a distinct and significant perspective in assessing CSW performance. Audience does not necessarily imply a dependency relationship, as does the term "client," nor does it refer exclusively to responsibility, as does the notion, "constituency."(1) At this stage it simply serves to isolate what we anticipate to be distinct viewpoints on commission activities. In other words the audience concept organizes subjective perceptions of commission impact.

By approaching performance from an impact perspective, this chapter aims first to clarify the meaning that different commission audiences assign to effectiveness and second to explore context characteristics associated with variation in these forms of effective commission performance. Initially, however, the success of this analysis of commission performance requires the resolution of some knotty theoretical and methodological problems.

THEORETICAL AND METHODOLOGICAL CONCERNS

The organization theory literature presents two distinct conceptions of organizational effectiveness. The "system's resource" approach gauges organizational effectiveness in terms of the organization's interaction with its environment. The use of this model assumes that goals of organizations are simply not identifiable and that in fact the only empirically identifiable goal is organizational survival.(2) The alternative approach to organizational effectiveness focuses on goal attainment, i.e., the extent to which a unit is achieving its internally determined objectives.(3)

Adopting a definition of effectiveness for any particular research effort hinges on the nature of the organizational unit and the purposes of the research. The goal-attainment approach is appropriate where those individuals who establish the organizational objectives are a clearly identifiable group and where research is specifically concerned with "performance" in an area defined by that organization's formal raison d'etre. Commissions on the Status of Women meet these criteria: the commission leadership and staff form a clearly identifiable body of goal setters, and this research aims, in part, to analyze performance in terms of a commission's own priorities. In reference to the various modes of operationalizing performance, it is this focus on goal attainment that allows for the examination of the "impact" dimension of organizational performance in this study.

Within this context, gauging effectiveness requires explicit empirical identification of commission goals and measured assessment of commission effectiveness in achieving those goals.(4) Furthermore, the development of a common denominator in terms of goals would facilitate comparative analysis. The method of empirically identifying goal areas for commissions was discussed at length in chapter 3. In the five communities studied, commission leaders, including the CSW officers, chairpersons of major committees and professional staff, were asked to assign a value to each one of seven goal areas, on a scale from 1-5, ranging from "top importance" to "of no importance" to the commission. The goal areas had been constructed from the responses to a survey of local commissions and from information derived in the pretest conducted in one community.

Commission effectiveness was operationalized through adoption of an instrument developed by Georgopoulos and Mann in their study of community general hospitals.(5) In this study several groups within hospitals were asked to rate the programs with which they were familiar. The instrument thus allowed knowledgeable individuals to evaluate organizational performance in relation to organizational goals.

From the vantage point of studying Commissions on the Status of Women the limitation of this approach lies in the population selected to measure effectiveness. To assess the effectiveness of an organization in terms of its impact (attainment of objectives beyond self-serving organizational ones), one must go beyond organization members to the audiences of the organization. Admittedly, Georgopoulos and Mann queried persons within the organization because only these individuals were thought to be sufficiently knowledgeable to evaluate performance; but ideally one would identify individuals who were both knowledgeable and external to the unit under study. While hospital studies may be more resistant to such designs, Commissions on the Status of Women as organizations can readily be assessed through the eyes of external audiences, as long as the criterion of "knowledgeable individuals" can be met. This approach is particularly well suited to a study framed around in-depth interviews, because the goals of the organization can be clearly specified and informed external assessors easily identified.

External audiences, with whose evaluation we are concerned, are drawn from both the community and the local government itself. Those individuals selected from the community represented distinct constituency audiences. A constituency audience is an audience to which a commission may be responsible in some representational sense.(6) The two constituency audiences tapped in all communities were the "reformist-activist" and the "feminist-activist." The reformist-activist perspective was provided by the League of Women Voters president in each community. The feminist-activist was provided by the National Organization for Women convener in four of the five communities, and by the Women's Political Caucus chairperson in one community. While it can be assumed that both the reformist and the feminist are concerned with women's issues, the assessment of commission effectiveness might vary depending on the image of acceptable level and kinds of impact held by each. In four of the five communities, a "nonmainstream" feminist contingent played a prominent role in the indigenous women's organizational network. They include leaders of lesbian organizations, ethnic organizations, welfare mothers and peer counseling groups. For purposes of this analysis these nonmainstream audiences are grouped together in order to highlight the clearly shared elements in their assessment of commission effectiveness.

Local officials comprise the internal audience whose assessment counts in analyzing commission effectiveness. Both those public officials to whom commissions report and those who share similar functional responsibilities inside local government provide informed and distinct perspectives on commission effectiveness. In each community the chief executive officer - or, in cases where the chief executive officer did not meet the "informed" criteria, the highest ranking informed executive officer in the jurisdiction - was interviewed. This included all of the mayors, the chief administrative officers, and two budget directors. In addition the head of the unit with general responsibility for implementation of civil rights laws was interviewed, in order to provide the civil rights perspective from inside government. In three communities this was the executive director of a human relations-type citizen board. In two communities this person was the head of a human relations department.

Given that these are the relevant audiences for the local Commission on the Status of Women, how does one calculate their relative assessments of commission effectiveness? Following a modified Georgopoulos and Mann approach, I calculated respondent assessment of commission effectiveness by taking an average of the summed differences between the commission's own assessment of the importance of goal activities to it as a unit and the external respondents' assessment of commission effectiveness on that goal activity. The lower the index score for a particular commission, via a particular external respondent, the higher the overall effectiveness assessment for that commission from the audience perspective. The original questions, from which these importance ratings were derived, asked commission members to rank each goal area on an importance scale from 1 to 5 and asked each audience informant to assess the effectiveness of the commission in each of the seven goal areas, using a 1 to 5 effectiveness scale. Figure 5.1 represents audience assessment of effectiveness by community.

See Appendix A for the interview schedule. If a person interviewed as representing a particular audience indicated that she/he could not make a judgment about the effectiveness of the commission in some goal-activity area, this was treated as missing data and the number of activity areas by which the summed score was divided was reduced accordingly. This adjustment was made to avoid treating lack of judgment as a negative assessment of the commission.

When using index scores derived in this fashion, reliability of the result increases as one moves toward the end points on the continuum of high to low effectiveness. Thus in this effort to generate an understanding of both the content of effective action and the conditions producing "effective" commissions of various kinds, we focus largely on the "high" and "low" cases as viewed from the vantage point of the informants from each audience.

Community

Maryville County   EX*   CR*   RA   FA
                                                                         (1.68)   (1.95)

Onega   CR EX*   FA   NMA* RA
                  (0.06)   (.56)   (1.55)
                   RA
                  (0.04)

Dodge County   CR   CR   EX   NMA FA
                  (0.07)   (0.91) (1.06)   (1.62) (1.63)

Altona   FA EX   RA   NMA
                          (0.53)(0.55)   (1.38)   (1.55)

St. George County EX   FA NMA   RA   CR
                  (-.52)   (0.94)(1.04)   (1.23)   (1.87)

        -0.50 -0.25   0.0   0.25   0.50   0.75   1.00   1.25   1.50   1.75   2.00
        High   Low

                           Effectiveness Scores

                    Symbol Key: EX = Executive officer
                                   CR = Civil rights officer
                                   RA = Reformist-activist
                                   FA = Feminist-activist
                                   NMA = Nonmainstream activist

*Estimation based on narrative
of interview; respondents unable
to use scoring scheme.

Fig. 5.1. Audience assessment of effectiveness.

84

THE EXECUTIVE OFFICER VIEWPOINT

From the vantage point of executive leadership - elected and nonelected - the image of commission performance is shaped largely by its executive director. (In one community where the commission had no formal executive director the chairperson of the commission functioned in this role. The executive officials interviewed focused on her in their discussion of the commission.) The most favorable assessment from this perspective is found in St. George County. Here the executive officer sees the commission as a powerful and well-organized pressure group that has the capacity to pressure from both inside and outside government. He reports that the commission enjoys a constituency both strong and broad based. To be sure, he recognizes that the commission does have opposition in the community; but he perceives that opposition as rooted in substantive disagreement with commission values, rather than in dissatisfaction with commission performance in a procedural sense. As illustrative of CSW power, he notes that while the human relations commission and the Commission on the Status of Women should, from a pure management perspective, be under one body, this would not be politically feasible because the capacity of the Commission on the Status of Women's executive director to muster external support is too substantial.

The high marks which the executive official in St. George County gives to this commission are not based purely on the political muscle it seemingly exercises. He reports that, in addition to strong organization and political clout, "this commission is one in which hard work is the rule." He recalls several specific instances in which the "hard work," especially of the staff, resulted in discernible change in substantive policy areas. Credit and lending discrimination are cited as a specific issue area in which the impact of commission action is well recognized. (One interesting side note is that as long as the CSW appears to be producing an impact in its priority areas it does not damage its image by increased funding requests. The St. George commission even has gained credibility with county officials by being aggressive about finding money outside of the budget, e.g., from a local needs assessment project, from a grant made available by the federal government, etc.)

The local executive official in Dodge County focused on the same general topics in elaborating his rationale for the relatively dim view he takes on CSW effectiveness there. First he perceives the commission as representing only a small segment of the community, roughly comparable in resources and breadth to the constituency of the advisory council on the arts, or the advisory board on migrant problems. This image sharply contrasts with his view of the human relations commission, which he portrays as representing the whole community. In terms of commission activity, this official gives the CSW low marks on its capacity to pursue its objectives either within the bureaucracy or through the elected board. He perceives the commission as unsophisticated in terms of the local political processes, suggesting that they clearly "need to learn to strategize better." Asserting that the commission has in the past made demands that were not politically feasible, he feels it has lost credibility with elected and administrative officials alike.

Juxtaposing the observations offered by the executive officials in each of these communities gives content to the meaning of commission effectiveness from the executive official perspective. Executive officials view commissions as effective if 1) they are perceived to represent organized political resources in the community, 2) they have had a successful track record in implementing their objectives through other units of government or private institutions, 3) they make demands that can be politically acceded to, and 4) they are perceived as reasonable to work with, that is, well prepared and knowledgeable. These findings generally corroborate findings reported elsewhere about official assessment of citizen activist groups.(7)

Given this substantive content of effectiveness from the "official" perspective, which elements of commission structure or process might suggest a basis for variation in official assessment? In comparing St. George and Dodge County we see commissions that are similar in a number of ways. The local governments are organized under the council-manager model and the executive directors in each community are administratively under the county executive. Both commissions began without executive directors and made a case to support the request for staff in stages. As well, both of the executive directors have been in their positions for at least three years and have, in large part, shaped their own role definitions. The commissions share a noncohesive membership, marked by internal racial and/or ethnic cleavages. Finally the commissions both operate in a political environment where opposition to commission values routinely emerges concurrent with periods of high commission visibility.

The major distinguishing mark is the way the executive director of each Commission on the Status of Women defines and plays her role. In St. George the executive director shares with the executive official the view that, as Commission staff, she is only administratively responsible to the manager's office. In fact, the executive official reported that when the commission staff was first hired the manager's office did not want any responsibility for it. The general consensus was that the staff was put under the county manager by the county council, in spite of the manager's reluctance, "because some of the council members wanted him to keep an eye on them." A roughly similar rationale led to the location of commission staff members in the Dodge County administrative structure. However, in St. George County, that attitude of the manager's office that evolved over time was, "Okay . . . you're really on your own. You're going to get political direction from the Commission on the Status of Women. Don't expect us [manager's office] to bail you out if you get into trouble."

The role definition that the executive director of the St. George commission brought to her job clearly fostered the evolution of this attitude. She sees herself as an initiator and a leader. From her perspective the somewhat ambiguous character of the authority relationships involved in having two bosses, the commission and the county manager, is something to capitalize on rather than to endure. In Dodge County, on the other hand, the county manager's office exercises substantial control over the current executive director. Her predecessor, the first executive director of the commission, had been "too activist" in the eyes of county management. When she resigned her position a few years ago, the executive officer handpicked the current director, stressing to her the need for a substantially more restricted role. County management told the current director pointedly that her job was to keep the CSW "out of trouble" and "in line." However, in terms of the way in which county management itself assesses commission effectiveness, the cost of following that job description appears to be high.

The executive director in St. George County aggressively pursues an advocate rather than a neutral-bureaucratic role. She acts with some security because her personal power base is in the community, where she maintains strong ties with the bar association, the local newspapers, and a major local university. The director's carefully cultivated media image, communicated as well to county management, is that of a fair, committed, tough advocate for county women. Because her power base is external, she is relatively free to develop a clear notion of CSW objectives and the means for achieving them independent of management policy.

In Dodge County the power base of the executive director is inside the bureaucracy. A high-ranking administrative official who covers the human services area for the county manager has been her mentor and reinforces the restricted role she plays. The role definition she accepts calls largely for carrying out the administrative detail of the commission operation and serving as a kind of buffer between the citizen commissioners and the county bureaucracy. Substantively her advice includes suggestions to tone down requests put to the county, to maintain a low public visibility on controversial

issues, and to remain satisfied with the covert, existing means
of securing county funding.   The director acknowledges that
an overriding theme in much advice she gives to the commissioners is her concern with "downside risk." The executive
director, in sum, does not see her role as creating issues or
bringing new issues to the attention of the commission, but
rather as guiding the commission to stress politically and
administratively feasible endeavors.   This role definition in
concept and practice flows directly from the power base of
the executive director.   Since her power base is located inside
the bureaucracy, an advocacy role, entailing an inevitable
clash with management values, seems unfeasible.   This fact
leads the executive director in Dodge County into an inevitable
bureaucratic Catch-22, as is suggested by a comparison of role
orientations and bureaucratic responses to these orientations in
Dodge and St. George counties.

    The executive director who develops a power base outside
of the county/city bureaucracy and who takes the lead in
defining issues and implementing solutions within the sphere of
commission action seems more capable of scoring high on those
elements that executive officials report as constituting effective
action.   She is more capable of convincing officials that she
represents a community interest.   Because she is relatively
autonomous and has clearly defined objectives, she can build
up a better track record in negotiations with other local
officials and units frustrating attainment of women's interests
in the community.   Still this independence does not detract
from her capacity to shape demands so that they can be met or
to communicate a well-prepared and knowledgeable image.

    A "team-player" role orientation of the executive director
thus seems disfunctional.   It may be especially so where the
version of team policy filters through second-level officials in
the manager's office.   Certainly in the Dodge County case, the
deputy county manager, who served as the mentor of the CSW
executive director, had a substantially more restricted view of
the degree of advocacy appropriate than did other local
officials, including the county manager.   In short, while the
"team player" might make bureaucratic friends, the more
activist executive director influences people. When officials
look at CSW effectiveness it is influencing people that counts.
(The one exception to this rule occurs when the executive
official holds as high priority the enactment of a women's
agenda as defined by the local Commission on the Status of
Women.   When this kind of dovetailing of interests takes place
the team-player model might lead to a high effectiveness rating
from the executive official perspective.)

THE CIVIL RIGHTS ENFORCEMENT VIEWPOINT

From the vantage point of the civil rights officer, the citizen board itself is the focus in evaluating Commissions on the Status of Women. To a much greater extent than general management executive officials, civil rights officers inside local government place value on volunteer citizen boards and commissions. Stemming from their typical involvement with change efforts in the civil rights movement, these officials recognize the assistance such commissions can provide in mobilizing outside, grass-roots pressure to further change. Thus they view citizens' boards in an instrumental fashion, as affording the opportunity to capitalize on the relative freedom from "official" constraints such bodies enjoy. Citizens, rather than staff, on such commissions hold the key to mobilizing outside pressure. Civil rights officials, in short, define effectiveness in terms of capacity for catalyzing community action.

The most favorable assessment of commission effectiveness came from the human relations department head in Onega. Effectiveness for him means mobilization of citizen interest:

> The only role the Commission [on the Status of Women] has performed effectively is the acting as a conduit that takes those needs and concerns and acts then as a catalyst to see them implemented or handled. That's about all an advisory group can do in government . . . and once they try to do more than that, they're absolutely powerless.

The catalytic action deemphasizes direct lobbying from within bureaucracy by the executive director. Lobbying should always be indirect and accomplished through energizing unorganized and organized community interests. Another executive director illustrates the same point by this example:

> Let's say government is considering establishing a policy with regard to employment of women. It would be better for the commission to act to energize other organizations [who, in turn] . . . petition law makers, petition the mayor, in other words, do whatever would insure success.

The civil rights officer in Dodge County offered the least favorable assessment of commission effectiveness, her definition of effectiveness being identical to that suggested by her counterpart in Onega. She saw an effective commission as one which could "organize grass-roots client-group activity." From her own vantage point as one who works with a citizens'

board, she perceived the great advantage of citizens' involvement on boards and commissions as being relative freedom
from bureaucratic restraints.   Citizens' borad members with
organizational ties to the community can use those ties to
mobilize widespread support for action in some commission-
defined priority areas.   The failure of the Dodge County CSW
in this area leads to her low assessment of its effectiveness.

In summary, both civil rights officials define effectiveness
for the CSW in terms of mobilizing community groups in
support of the commission agenda.   An effective commission
taps a wide range of women's interest groups, represents their
interests in formulating the commission agenda, and brings
these community groups into the policy process, especially at
the critical decision-making and implementation stages.   Given
this definition of effectiveness, what element of commission
structure or process might suggest a basis for variation in
civil rights official assessment?

Both of these commissions are large, with memberships of
over 25, and both are highly dependent on committees for the
generation and promotion of ideas.   The executive director in
each case describes her role as "supportive and responsive"
rather than "leading."   One procedural feature, however, does
seem to distinguish the two commissions.   In identifying
citizens for appointment to open slots on the commission, the
search procedures followed produce two different results in
terms of the segment of the community represented by the
commission membership.

In both Onega and Dodge elected officials appoint commission members. In Dodge, each council member and the
mayor appoint three members to the commission.   In Onega,
the mayor makes all of the commission appointments.   In each
case nominations are controlled somewhat by an informal
agreement between the executive director and the elected
official, both of whom agree to comply where possible with
recommendations made by the commission.   The Dodge County
executive director reports the procedure typically works like
this:

> If somebody [an elected official] has an opening
> I'll just call and say [to the assistant], "If Commis-
> sioner Smith doesn't have somebody specific in mind,
> we have really heard of a fantastic person who's
> very interested.   Maybe he would want to consider
> her."   Sometimes they do and sometimes they don't.

Both executive directors report that the nature of the informal
procedure varies with the elected official.   The Onega executive director explains:

It depends upon who is mayor. Mayor Jones wanted several recommendations and he would appoint generally from among them. [With another mayor] you would go down to the mayor's office and say, "We have four openings, and here are four letters of appointment with resumes attached."

If each commission, through its executive director, has a substantial impact on its own composition, the difference between the two lies in how this prerogative is used. Both commissions report their desire for broad community involvement; the selection criteria implicitly operating in Onega favors grass-roots involvement, however, while that operating in Dodge militates against it.

In Onega individuals are recommended for appointment to the commission only after they have proven their commitment and competency through service on a task force or subcommittee of the commission. Each of the eight committees has a series of smaller work groups consisting of interested persons from the community. Typically the commission chairperson asks the chairpersons of the committees to recommend persons from the community who have worked effectively on a CSW committee and who have expressed interest in becoming a member of the commission. This is the pool from which the recommendations are drawn. Such a criterion produces a commission membership which does not reflect the community elite. As one politically active woman described the CSW with some disdain: "It is a commission of 'nonheavies' in terms of the community." However, the members are people who have become personally concerned about some problem women face and who have worked hard, through the commission, to find a solution.

In Dodge County, on the other hand, the premium is on public image. Names suggested by the commission are drawn from a pool of people who are already relatively well known in the community. The recent reappointment to the commission of the chamber of commerce executive director demonstrates the premium placed on achieving representation of a community elite. Originally appointed with the strong endorsement of commission leadership, this member of the local business elite became chairperson of the employment task force. A fellow commissioner described the new appointee's perspective on affirmative action as: "Wait a minute! When it comes to the employment of a person in a job you're going too far [with affirmative action]. Don't tell me who I can hire!" Smiling, the commissioner I interviewed reassured me, "We're all going to change that attitude if we live long enough." Whether in fact this man will be resocialized through his work with the commission remains problematic. Clearly his reappointment to the commission, through the advocacy of the chairperson,

illustrates how high a value this commission places on maintaining elite representation in the membership.

To summarize, the primary criterion for effectiveness
used by the civil rights officers is the extent to which the
commissions can mobilize grass-roots community groups to
pressure for enactment of the commission agenda. Reflecting
on the two cases examined here, this goal seems best served
by selecting membership based on performance in some substantive area of concern. This procedure taps individuals
linked to groups that can be mobilized readily on specific
issues. The commission that looks first at the general elite
status of members, in the hope of socializing these individuals
to a concern with matters on the CSW agenda, has expended
considerable energy without much result. Furthermore, even
if in some cases this strategy might succeed, the elites would
probably not have the grass-roots ties which, from a civil
rights perspective, motivate the necessary pressure for change
in this area.

Thus far we have focused on defining and accounting
for effectiveness as viewed from inside government. These
perceptions presumably shape the way in which internal
resources are distributed, to the benefit or detriment of the
local CSW. But a second set of assessments comes from an
external constituency and fits more conventional conceptions
about the proper jurors of performance for citizen boards and
commissions. In this case, the women's organizational activists
throughout the community comprise the relevant external constituency. As indicated earlier, specific activists were selected
in each community to represent the "reformist," the "feminist,"
and in four of the five communities the "nonmainstream"
perspectives.

THE REFORMIST-ACTIVIST VIEWPOINT

The president of the League of Women Voters (LWV) in each
community provided the reformist organizational perspective.
This perspective seemed substantially less susceptible to
variation in response to differing commission behavior and
styles of action. In four of the five communities the LWV
president reported a relatively low assessment of commission
effectiveness. Only in one community was a high rating of the
commission provided.

From this reformist perspective, effective action has
style, issue, and impact elements. An effective commission is
one in which members and staff employ a nonirritating interpersonal style in order to achieve well-defined and significant
policy objectives. All four of the commissions scoring low from
the reformist viewpoint were criticized because commission

members were naive in their lobbying endeavors or because they did not put enough effort into lobbying. The LWV presidents perceived CSW goal-setting processes as inadequate, uniformly deriding the commissions for allowing heated conflicts to flare up in their groups. Finally they expressed concern that, as an outcome of that process, the wrong issues were stressed. The reformists chided the commissions for going off on one tangent after another, rather than promoting important policy matters with which local government can deal and doggedly pursuing those issues to a favorable outcome.

Listening to these descriptions of what constitutes effectiveness for a commission, one is struck by the extent to which the LWV organization itself is the prototype being used. When this point was raised with one LWV president, she admitted the similarity but distinguished between the commission and the LWV roles in terms of issue emphasis and vantage point: "The Commission on the Status of Women should be an advocate within government. [It should play] the burr under the saddle function on women's issues." Another president answered that the commission's role was "pressing the government from within to do things for women." This role the LWV could not and should not take on.

Given this definition of commission effectiveness what characteristics of the Dodge County commission led its local League of Women Voters president to give it high marks? As noted above, the four other commissions, uniformly rated low from the reformist vantage point, vary in many ways. They are staffed and unstaffed; they are citizen dominant and staff dominant; they are large and small; they have from 25 to 0 percent commissioners with League of Women Voter backgrounds. None of these factors group together in a way to distinguish these commissions from the Dodge County commission. Instead, the critical factor informing reformist assessment of effectiveness appears to be some combination of the organizational and membership factors that produces a peculiar organizational style.

The community "notable" criterion, which the Dodge County commission uses to guide designation of new members, operates most rigorously in the selection of committee chairpersons. People are asked to serve as chairpersons because they are established and well known in the community, with the underlying assumption being that their own personal weight will further CSW lobbying efforts. Each of the task force chairpersons interviewed reported that when action in some area was needed, he/she as an individual went directly to the local official who could service that request. Their operational style was basically one on one. There was no thought of mobilizing outside pressure of any kind; these chairpersons seemed to assume that by virtue of their prestige, the power of their arguments would prevail.

When the LWV president gave the Dodge commission high marks, her focus seemed to be on this organizational style. The Dodge CSW reflected a LWV style of operation, inside government, to a much greater extent than did other commissions. Of course, the recruitment procedure, by which the CSW chairperson appointed to leadership positions community notables, produced this style. This sense, that if the style is correct the organization is having about as much impact as it can have, came through clearly from the interview with the LWV president. The fact that a recruitment process which weighs heavily on the side of community prominence might lead to a nonfeminist commission membership is a price that this reformist seems willing to pay, presumably because she has a somewhat unidimensional model of effective action. An effective commission is one on which the commissioners and staff bring to the position the confidence and weight to perform, on the inside, a role paralleling the LWV action on the outside.

The irony emerging from this analysis is that heavy emphasis on community influentials in leadership roles found in Dodge County is directly related to the civil rights officer's low assessment of the CSW in that community. Grass-roots power, the mark of highly effective commission from the civil rights official perspective, seems to short-circuit community influential leadership on CSW.

THE FEMINIST-ACTIVIST VIEWPOINT

The feminist perspective was provided by the National Organization for Women (NOW) convener in four of the communities and by the chairpersons of the Women's Political Caucus (WPC) in the fifth. Virtually all persons interviewed agreed that these individuals represented the feminist group perspective of their community.

Again the three questions guiding this analysis are: 1) How is effectiveness defined by the feminists in the high and low effectiveness communities? 2) Is this definition of effectiveness uniform across all of the feminists interviewed? and 3) What factors seem to account for high and low ratings assigned to commissions?

To a feminist, an effective Commission on the Status of Women is one actively concerned with the whole realm of women's needs, including "liberation issues." Its major function is to legitimize these issues in the community. In Marysville County, where the CSW scored lowest in NOW leadership eyes, the local convener reported:

> The Commission on the Status of Women is a
> service oriented group . . . and it's geared toward
> women, but I wouldn't call it feminist. . . . I'd like
> to see a more feminist orientation. . . . They [CSW]
> don't have a total grasp of women's needs because
> they are ignoring the feminist segment.

In Onega, where the NOW organization gave the Commission on
the Status of Women high marks on effectiveness, NOW saw the
commission as taking up feminist issues and giving them
credibility. The convener reported that, as a feminist leader
she valued the CSW as an instrument of power, adding: "An
effective commission legitimizes feminist interests." The
commission in Onega seemed capable of accomplishing this task.

Recent analyses of the women's movement generally
distinguish between its "women's rights" and the "women's
liberation" branches,(8) although at least one scholar asserts
that making such a distinction is futile.(9) The Commission on
the Status of Women and the more feminist NOW activists may
indeed represent these two branches. Certainly, in talking
with NOW activists about the commissions, the feminist-activist
sentiment comes through that Commissions on the Status of
Women are not strong enough on liberation issues. Tension
between the civil rights issues on the one hand, and liberation
issues on the other emerged in every NOW discussion of the
local CSW. Understandably different emphasis imposed
constraints on NOW members serving on commissions. A NOW
convener in St. George county put the problem in this way:

> NOW members are more or less outnumbered by
> those who see [the commission] . . . as their
> version of an organization for women's rights. To
> them it is not a feminist organization first, it is a
> women's organization, which is a difference . . .
> there are two kinds of issues: civil rights issues and
> feminist issues or liberation issues . . . on a scale
> of 1 to 10 they are nine on civil rights issues; on
> liberation issues they are somewhere around 4.

For the most part NOW members feel that a Commission on the
Status of Women should be a feminist, not simply a women's
rights organization. Their ideology, which insists that all
women are feminist at some level, bolsters this perspective: to
be a feminist organization is to represent all women.

What seems to differentiate commissions receiving high
and low ratings from this feminist-activist audience? The
major distinguishing characteristic appears to center on the
internal organizational process by which decisions are reached
and implemented. In all of the communities the CSW were
actively concerned with the issues that the NOW conveners

labeled as the most pressing feminist issues: rape, wife abuse, and employment, for example. But in the commission judged most effective, a high degree of openness characterized the decision process resulting in CSW involvement in these areas. The Onega commission, for example, reached its decisions about the nature and degree of CSW involvement in the wife abuse problem openly, airing the issue at a public meeting, and thus helping to draw public attention to the issue. In the commission judged least effective, the staff largely formulated and implemented CSW objectives in this area in a fairly in- visible fashion. Both processes, incidentally, resulted in productive actions.

Presumably, the Onega commission lost some credibility with public officials by using an open process to decide their action on the wife abuse problem. Disorderly and apparently uncontrolled meetings seldom impress conflict-shy public administrators. However, that open process provided a public forum for addressing a significant feminist issue, with the fact that the forum itself is an official governmental commission lending credibility to such issues. Stressing the importance of this legitimizing role the NOW convener in Onega explained: "If the Commission on the Status of Women says something about what is going on in one of these areas [wife abuse, rape, etc.] people might pay attention. If NOW says it's going on they say, 'That's just a bunch of radical women again.'"

In sum, to gain positive assessment from a feminist- activist perspective a CSW must not only represent a feminist agenda but also reach decisions concerning implementation of that agenda through a very public process. In the words of one feminist-activist from Dodge County, "They must be willing to bite the bullet . . . to call the question, to challenge." From the feminist perspective the process itself promotes the agenda.

THE NONMAINSTREAM ACTIVIST VIEWPOINT

In four of the five communities some women's activist groups represented specialized women's interests. Such groups are labeled "nonmainstream" because they depart from the broader perspective of both the reformists and feminist activists in their communities, in terms of both problem focus and solutions generated. In two communities lesbian groups were quite strong; in two communities ethnic women's organizations were growing in strength; in one community third world/low-income women were mobilized and demanding recognition; in another welfare mothers were regrouping after a long period of disorganization. Without question these nonmainstream groups gave low marks to the Commissions on the Status of Women.

Hence, in these cases some merit lies in drawing out some of the constituent elements of effectiveness common to each of these perspectives and then exploring factors militating against CSWs conforming to this notion of effectiveness.

These "out" groups seemed to define effectiveness in rather narrow and issue-specific terms. All of these groups view their respective CSW as deficient. Groups representing low-income and ethnic women saw removal of this deficiency as possible through the commission becoming more responsive to them. Those groups taking this position set a very high standard of "responsiveness." The representative of each organization felt that the commissions should be promoting - as a major concern - the issue around which her own group was currently mobilized. This often was generalized to a critique of the brand of feminism promoted by the Commission on the Status of Women. One leader of an organization for low-income women criticized the middle-class, protected feminism of her commission. She reported: "I'm a feminist, but . . . if I'm going to devote my life and my energy to helping women, I'm going to start with the most disadvantaged of the disadvantaged." The commission, she felt, focused on liberal issues and never really reached problems faced by the most disadvantaged women. She expressed particular disdain for a recent effort on the part of the CSW to have county job titles changed.

> I really feel that they should get down to the issues that affect the majority of women. . . . Unenforced child support laws are one of the worst examples of sex discrimination and . . . running around changing the word "fireman" to "firefighter" is not going to get child support checks for these women to feed their children. I don't think they [CSW] see it [unenforced child support] as sex discrimination. I see it as sex discrimination, because if men were waiting for the check, the D.A. would process it a lot faster.

While the matter of what concerns should be at the core of feminism varied somewhat, from the nonmainstream perspective the assessment of the local CSW as deficient on this score is constant. Even the lesbian activists, who recognized the commission could not deal with lesbian issues, faulted it for ignoring other most important questions.

It was not the substantive matters alone that led to the distance between local CSW and these groups. Traits common to each of these groups were that they were not especially well organized; they had considerable conflict within their own membership; and they were grass roots in a 1960s sense. From their perspective the CSW style of operation seemed overly professionalized, if not colonial. Altona illustrates this problem particularly well.

In Altona the CSW is dominated by women who are in the leadership of the women's movement in the state. From this vantage point they can function effectively in agenda building and gain favorable evaluations from feminist activists in the community and the civil rights establishment alike in terms of overall effectiveness. But this style of operation has its costs. Because the professional women's movement leadership of the commission knows how to do things to produce results, input from less "professionalized" commission members diminishes and input from nonprofessionalized activist groups, like ethnics and lesbians, disappears entirely. The non-mainstream activists, while admitting agreement with the outcome of many commission efforts, resent the elitist notions motivating those efforts. They distrust the decisions about priorities that are made in an elitist system, even if the elites are certified feminists.

To illustrate this point, one leader of a large ethnic women's organization described her involvement in a public hearing that was held by the CSW to gather needs information on women in the community. First, she reported, the agenda for the hearing was set by the commission leadership, who sought testimony on the plight of low-income and ethnic women from social welfare professionals. When a leader of the major local ethnic women's organization heard of the hearing, she demanded places on the agenda for some of the women she represented in the ethnic community. The commission graciously agreed to the addition but, having already set the schedule, they placed most of the women from this group at the end of the list of witnesses. By the time the ethnic women were heard most of the audience, including city council members, had gone home. The ethnic group leader put her reaction to this series of events quite simply: the CSW may be feminist, "but they just don't understand colonialism."

Since across the five communities studied, nonmainstream groups never gave high marks to a commission, it is difficult to construct a picture of a context likely to produce such an assessment. The only clear finding is negative: commissions conducting their affairs in a highly professionalized fashion, even though the commission may be staunchly feminist and unambiguously citizen based, will come to loggerheads with leaders in traditional grass-roots organizations.

The aphorism "Where you stand depends on where you sit,"(10) familiar to students of organization theory, best describes the differences found in the scorekeeping of various CSW audiences. The location of a particular audience, in the policy system, has much to do with its priorities and perceptions, and thus much to do with its judgment of local CSW effectiveness. Informants from the management (executive officials), civil rights and reformists activist groups share both a background of concern with a wide range of issues and a stress on the process aspects of effectiveness. However, the content of that process constituting effectiveness varies: for management it is reasonable, competent, impact-oriented staff behavior; for civil rights officials it is a capacity for catalyzing community action; for the reformist-activist it is maintaining a nonirritating lobbying style directed toward a clear objective. The feminist-activist and nonmainstream activists are concerned less with process and more with the impact of commission action. To the former effectiveness means legitimizing liberation issues in the community; to the latter it implies impacting on areas of concern to them, narrowly defined. This distinction between process and impact, in defining commission effectiveness, may reside simply in the single- versus multi-issue concerns of the two sets of groups, a point illustrating the "where you stand depends on where you sit" aphorism.

Given that the structures and processes of local Commissions on the Status of Women are somewhat malleable, what does this analysis suggest about the range of commission choices? Can a commission serve multiple audiences by conforming to multiple notions of effectiveness? Clearly some of these definitions of effectiveness are compatible with one another. A commission can have a strong, competent, impact-oriented staff which shares with commission members a nonirritating interpersonal style directed toward clear objectives, thus responding to both management and reformist norms. Similarly the civil rights officials' criterion of grassroots involvement fits comfortably with the legitimation of liberation issues, the standard of the feminist activist.

Striking incompatibilities exist, however, in organizational variables apparently associated with different definitions of effectiveness. The grass-roots selection criterion, associated with the capacity for mobilizing community action favored by the civil rights officials, contradicts the premium placed by the reformist-activist on achieving representation of community elites. Likewise the open, conflictual, and disorderly decision-making process leading to legitimizing liberation issues, espoused by feminist activists, runs counter to a strong independent staff, the phenomenon associated with effectiveness from management's perspective.

In short, this comparative study implies a second aphorism, "You can't please all of the people all of the time," suggesting that commissions may have some difficult choices to make. In terms of the "effectiveness" dimension of performance, local Commissions on the Status of Women would be well advised to reflect on both the audience with whom they want to score high, and the aspects of their own operations that might best serve that objective.

6 The Women's Movement: Organizing Change and Evaluating Institutions

How do we evaluate the role which local Commissions on the Status of Women play in advancing the change objectives of the women's movement? Initially we recognize change as a neutral term suggesting very different directions. Positive change implies movement toward wider distribution of goods and services in a society, greater sharing of political power, and enlarged opportunities for human development. Negative change suggests narrower distribution and increased constraints in each of these categories, with intensified defense of the status quo.(1) This analysis of women's movement organizations only considers positive change objectives; accordingly it explores the role of Commissions on the Status of Women in securing redistribution of goods and services, political power, and opportunity for individual development. In terms of this objective the question becomes: Do commissions merit the substantial commitment of activist resources evident in many communities, or should they be abandoned, as some critics suggest, as serving mainly to preserve the status quo?

The discussion in this concluding chapter presumes that a meaningful answer to this question will emerge only after a more theoretical analysis of how positive change is realized. Thus the first step is to examine alternative models describing the dynamics of political and policy change, and highlighting the criteria by which each model assesses performance. Next the Commission on the Status of Women change efforts are evaluated in the context of the pluralist-politics model - that model most fitting its organization. Then typical activities organized under the two remaining change models, the protest model and the bureaucratic model, are juxtaposed to the CSW mode. Finally a way of thinking about the allocation of women's movement resources is discussed - a discussion which leads to a future research agenda.

100

PLURALISM AND POSITIVE CHANGE

Pluralism holds that democracy is best preserved in a political system where multiple, competing elites offer voters meaningful choices in elections and where new elites can gain access to political decision-making power.(2)   Fragmentation of power is thus a central component of pluralist thinking. This model of politics assumes transitory "elites" and "nonelites," with power shifting from group to group, issue by issue.   Individuals participating in decisions at one point in time do not necessarily participate at another point in time.   The theory assumes that most citizens do have the opportunity to exercise power, whether they choose to do so or not. Level of concern distinguishes those who participate and have influence from those who do not.   Once sufficiently concerned about a set of issues, citizens gain access to the political decision-making system simply by acquiring the skills of leadership.(3)

In this view of the political system, political change comes about through new groups or interests acquiring the skill of leadership and making their interests known at election time. Given leadership and organization previously ignored groups in the society can shape political decision making in line with their own objectives.

PROTEST AND POSITIVE CHANGE

Many observers of politics in America would argue that the pluralist model simply doesn't describe reality.(4)   They assert instead that the opportunities or resources necessary for producing change are exclusively distributed, with certain groups remaining disadvantaged over long periods of time.   To these powerless groups protest activity is the only viable alternative to pluralist politics.

The protest mode of political action is oriented toward repudiation of public policies or social conditions and is characterized by showmanship or demonstration of an unconventional kind.(5)   Assuming that pluralist politics maps strategy only for those already working effectively with the system, the protest model offers guidelines to those striving to create political resources. It suggests two broad bases on which such resources might be grounded.   One is simply negative inducement. A group may seek by public display or disruptive acts to raise the cost to another party of continuing a certain course of action.(6)   Change is secured as a result of this negative inducement, i.e., the protest action creates "a state of affairs distasteful to the target organization and for the cessation of which it is willing to make concessions."(7)

Powerless groups might also use positive inducements to bring about change. Lipsky stresses these in his description of how powerless people can employ protest to activate "third parties" to enter "the implicit or explicit bargaining arena in ways favorable to the protestors." Under this model change comes about when these third parties, who are powerful, champion the cause of powerless groups. Whether the focus is on negative inducements or gaining the support of external publics the general purpose is the same: protest is a strategy utilized by relatively powerless groups in order to increase their bargaining ability.

BUREAUCRACY AND POSITIVE CHANGE

The third model change through bureaucracy rejects the classic "truth" of the separation of political decision making and administration. Rather the model assumes that bureaucracy really controls the policy process, with most political decision making today occurring in this realm. Since, it is argued, the focus of political power has shifted away from the electoral and legislative arena, traditional notions of representativeness and accountability as well as strategies for securing these values need to be rethought. In short, change today comes about through bureaucratic action. Hence both pluralist and protest models miss the mark by ignoring the centrality of bureaucracy.(8)

One recent work on bureaucracy focused on several factors which contributed to bringing about this shift. First, general changes in society have produced a heightened legitimacy for those who profess a kind of neutral competence - the hallmark of the professional bureaucrat. Additionally, the amount of attention that elected officials are able to give any particular problem is both scarce and inherently serial in nature. Bureaucrats, on the other hand, with their specialized interests can focus attention on a much narrower range of issues. Thus, specialized knowledge, a prolonged attention span, and the premium placed on innovation in the society generally, gives professionalized public bureaucrats an unmatched capacity to initiate and innovate in that they dominate the creation, analysis and transformation of information. The alternatives from which the elected political actors select are created by the bureaucrat. This means, in effect, that bureaucrats are in a position to compete for the allocation of scarce resources and at the same time provide the criteria on which allocation decisions are made.(9) Securing change obviously necessitates breaking into the bureaucratic decision-making process.

In addition to simply describing how change occurs in the political system these three models carry implicit criteria for assessing action on behalf of new groups. As might be anticipated from their divergent conceptions of the instrument of change, the models employ diverse criteria for measuring success.

Pluralism

As a process model, pluralism contains distinctive assessment criteria. Since the correctness of a particular action can not be established, attention focuses on the procedures through which change can take place. To merit favorable judgment from the pluralist perspective, a system would work toward establishing effective mechanisms for expressing preferences about direction of needed change. In the case of the women's movement, favorable evaluation would hinge on the extent to which a particular change-oriented activity produced or maintained a vehicle for the open expression of a wide range of women's preferences.

Protest

Protest theory offers two slightly different criteria for assessing success. One school sees protest as producing the basis for organization, which then becomes the lever for change. Protest is seized on whenever possible to organize people - for ultimately, "change comes from power, and power comes from organization. In order to act, people must act together . . . for no one can negotiate without the power to compel negotiation."(10) Protest provides occasion for organizing powerless women; organization is the criterion for assessing protest activity.

A second variation on the protest theme holds lower expectations. Here protest constitutes its own end. Piven and Cloward, most notably, argue that powerless people can disrupt (protest) but cannot control the response to the disruption. They must simply rely on the political rever- berations of their disruptions, which may be an especially productive strategy during periods of political and social instability. Disruption or protest becomes its own end. If a visible protest over a women's issue occurs the activity is judged positively.

Bureaucracy

Bureaucracy offers an outcome criterion for gauging the value
of an activity: a programmatic objective must be attained.
Programmatic objectives are clearly articulated by responsible
bureaucrats in particular areas who compete for resources
and supervise the implementation of these objectives. For
example the women's division in a department of human
services might be evaluated by the extent to which it meets
general programmatic objectives, such as monitoring the
treatment of women in county programs. A rape crisis
program might be judged by the extent to which it meets more
narrow objectives such as educating the public regarding rape
prevention and establishing a rape crisis line. Unlike in the
pluralist model where success referred to proper procedure or
in the protest model where success means a form of action,
success here demands attainment of clearly defined and
measurable objectives.

PLURALIST POLITICS IN ACTION:
COMMISSIONS ON THE STATUS OF WOMEN

Any fair evaluation of the relative merit in committing activist
resources to one type of organizational activity versus another
must first acknowledge the change model on which the activity
is premised. Commissions on the Status of Women, in both
their origins and continuing support are predicated on a
pluralist politics model of change. In fact the commission as
an institution in democratic politics is typically described as a
"pluralizing" force.(11) Moreover the theory supporting the
establishment of such citizen commissions has been that they
serve to supplement traditional institutions of policy making by
bringing new perspectives on issues through widened participation on the input side of the decision-making process.(12)
Commissions often create new elites by appointing them to
commissions in order to secure their issue input.
        The formal statements of elected officials, announcing the
appointment of CSW, read like textbook descriptions of
pluralist politics in action. President Kennedy, in appointing
the first Presidential Commission on the Status of Women noted
". . . we have by no means done enough to strengthen family
life and at the same time encourage women to make their full
contribution as citizens. . . . It is appropriate at this time
. . . to review recent accomplishments, and to acknowledge
frankly the further steps that must be taken. This is a task
for the entire nation."(13) In the words of its establishing
document the Kennedy commission aimed to lead the country
toward "assuring women the opportunity to develop their

capacities and fulfill their aspirations . . . ."(14) This same pluralist rationale accompanied the establishment of state and then local Commissions on the Status of Women. A charter member of one successful commissions put the pluralist rationale in a way that fits the typical pattern:

> One of the principle arguments in favor of creating such a commission here was the fact that [this] county . . . must utilize its human resources wisely. If woman power was being wasted or underutilized simply because of archaic attitudes on the part of employers, schools or women themselves - the entire society was losing valuable creative ability. . . .

Thus the local Commission on the Status of Women not only brings a new group into the pluralistic political process but also enriches that process by calling attention to new issues. The extent to which commissions reflect this pluralist predilection for introducing new elites into the system is highlighted by the official stress commissions place on diversity of membership. The Handbook of Commissions on the Status of Women, published by the umbrella associations for commissions, urges appointing officials to select membership from a wide range of economic and religious backgrounds, men and women, public and private organizations of various kinds. As noted earlier, the enactment documents of local commissions also frequently call explicitly for a membership drawn from a broad cross section of the community.

Naively following this broad representation advice has led many commissions to the brink of self-destruction, however, since extreme diversity often produces stalemate. Astute commissions and appointing officials soon learn that, while diversity is desirable, some basis for a shared orientation is essential if a new elite group is to function effectively in pluralist politics. This developing sophistication of commissioners and appointing officials alike clearly does not invalidate the central pluralist premise. Commissions on the Status of Women measure favorably by the yardstick of the pluralist model as long as they facilitate a process by which new elites - representative of emerging women's interest to the extent that effective presentation of a coherent perspective will allow - can raise new women's issues in a legitimate political forum.

Limitations of the Pluralist Model

Like pluralism as a change model, the Commission on the Status of Women as an institution also has a dark side. In order to maintain the "new elite" status, so central to success for the commission, both participants and issues are subjected to a kind of exclusionary screening device. Those specialized interests or particular issues perceived by this new elite as likely to jeopardize the promotion of a wide range of women's movement issues and programs receive little or no commission concern. Two cases, drawn from the in-depth commission studies, illustrate this point.

During a regular executive committee meeting of one highly successful commission, the executive director brought up a morning newspaper report to which the Commission on the Status of Women had been asked to respond. Two women from a very poor section of town were charged with manslaughter after their unattended preschool-age children died in a fire in a house the women shared. Three other women, representing these black welfare mothers, came to the commission seeking help, arguing that these women were victims of unequal justice - because they were female, black, and poor.

While there seemed to be broad agreement, though not consensus, among executive committee members on the assertion that if these women had not been poor and black they would have been charged only with neglect, the CSW decided not to get involved. The ostensible reasons for the decision were: 1) the commission didn't have all the facts and 2) the commission should not intervene in individual cases just because women may appear to be victimized. The welfare mother advocates who had come asking for help were told that a committee would study the matter but that the CSW would not take a position.

Clearly the executive committee believed that embroilment in a controversy of this kind could damage the entire commission program. For in this case the rightness or wrongness of government action in charging the mothers with manslaughter touched on deep, system-challenging questions: Can there be equal justice in a society when people experience such unequal life conditions? Would the fathers of these children have been similarly charged had they left them unattended for a period of time? Early chapters discussed the "watchdogging" activities of many commissions, yet active monitoring of governmental action rarely extends into such unsettling areas as these. For the Commission on the Status of Women to maintain itself as a vehicle for female citizen access to the community political decision-making system, it must necessarily refuse assistance to women presenting certain kinds of needs.

This first case focuses on issues with which an institution playing pluralist politics cannot deal. At times organizations threaten the capacity for Commissions on the Status of Women to stay in the pluralist politics game. In order to survive, the commissions must exclude such organized interests. A story, recounted by a leader of the lesbian collective in one of the communities studied, illustrates this point.

> One day Barbara [chairperson of the CSW]
> told me that the Commission on the Status of Women
> was going to put out a newsletter. . . . What they
> were going to carry was little short stories about
> women's groups. I said, "We [the lesbian organi-
> zation] would love to have a story in there, and I'll
> be glad to write it," . . . and she said: "I'll give
> you a call." The next thing I knew I got a copy of
> their newsletter. It had articles on women's groups,
> and nobody had contacted us.

As the story continued this woman described repeated attempts
to get the information into the CSW newsletter - each try
meeting with failure. "I still haven't figured out what hap-
pened to the newsletter," she reports, but "I have the feeling
that they definitely want to put forth an image that would be
acceptable to the community as a whole." While she may not
understand fully this particular case, this lesbian leader sees
clearly the overall picture. When playing by the rules of
pluralist politics, Commissions on the Status of Women can be
successful only by maintaining broad-based support in the
community. Such support at times may come at the expense of
denying ties to socially unacceptable sister organizations. To
act otherwise would nullify the raison d'etre for Commissions
on the Status of Women.
    Quite clearly the pluralist bias of commissions puts
constraints on the ways they carry out activities directed
toward women's movement objectives. Just as Schattschneider
told us in 1960 - that the chorus in the pluralist heaven sings
with a strong upper-class accent,(15) so the Commission on
the Status of Women speaks in tones modulated by middle-class
respectability. Neither poor, black welfare mothers who may
be victims of unequal justice, nor lesbians eager to publicize
their existence, fit into the CSW scheme.
    The Commissions on the Status of Women, premised on the
pluralist politics model, represent one form of activity organized to accomplish women's movement objectives. The other
models discussed above, change via protest and change via
bureaucracy, suggest alternative avenues for committing
activist resources.

PROTEST POLITICS: ISSUES FOR ORGANIZING

The protest model sees change coming about as the product of
conscious protest actions. Some see such actions leading to an
organization which can itself play pluralist politics and thus
effect change.(16)   Others see the very act of protest,
accompanied by some response from the powerful as the best

that the powerless can aim for and thus in itself becomes the
measure of change.(17)   The women's movement, since its
resurgence in the 1960s, has reflected periodic manifestations
of this form.   Perhaps the most visible protest of the early
days was that one organized around the Miss America Pageant
in 1968.   Women from Washington, D.C., New Jersey, and
Florida joined to protest the contest as degrading to women.
Much in the late sixties street theater style, the group
crowned a live sheep Miss America and participants were
encouraged to toss into a trash can instruments of female
torture--old bras, girdles, high-heeled shoes, etc.(18)

The protest action in this case was ad hoc and designed
to deal with a specific issue, but - in accord with the protest
model - organizers were trying as well to make a statement
about the relationship between social, political and economic
freedom.(19)   Other late sixties protest actions fit in the same
mold.(20)   The contemporary versions of protest within the
women's movement have been much more narrowly focused than
these earlier street activities, although the motivating force is
the same.   Typically organizers try to create new resources
and channels of action for dealing with a discontent about
public policy by mobilizing large numbers of people behind
some kind of disruption of established political institutions.

During this latter half of the 1970s protest actions have
been effectively organized in response to judicial and administrative official's treatment of female victims of violence.
Protest in defense of abused wives and rape victims gained
greatest national attention.   Several cases illustrate the point.

One evening in August of 1977 in Clementon, New Jersey,
a woman was arrested and charged with the murder of her
husband the same night she had been brutally beaten by him.
The woman had experienced repeated beatings throughout her
married life, yet her regular calls to the police had resulted
merely in the order that the husband should "leave the house
to cool off."   The abused wife pleaded not guilty and the
court eventually agreed to reduce her bail from $100,000 to
$45,000 under the stipulation that she receive psychiatric
treatment.

However, the case itself provided the spark igniting a
protest action.   Immediately after the woman's arrest a defense
committee formed and held a press conference to publicize the
unresponsiveness of the police department in this and other
similar cases.   Beyond calling attention to the inadequacy of
police response the committee hoped to educate the public to
the wife abuse phenomenon and to let other abused wives know
that there was support for them in the larger community.

This New Jersey case and a similar one decided in
Michigan (also 1977) became rallying points for feminists
nationwide to question the adequacy of both the administrative
(police) and judicial institutions for dealing with wife abuse.

Spokespersons in these protest efforts take the position that abused wives may be forced to murder because the community offers them no other way out of their misery.

Treatment of accused rapists and rape victims, especially in the courts, has provided a second major occasion for protest action. A typical protest action of this kind was occasioned, during the summer of 1977, by a decision of the California Court of Appeals in Los Angeles, overturning a guilty verdict in the rape of a woman hitchhiker. The rationale for this reversal - in part that "women hitchhikers should anticipate advances from men who pick them up,"and in part that the defendant had not used physical force to overpower the victim - fueled the protest.

Following by just a month a decision of a Madison, Wisconsin, judge to mete out minimal punishment to a 16-year-old boy who, "reacting normally to a sexually permissive community," raped a classmate, the Los Angeles decision highlighted the powerlessness of rape victims. The Madison case had created a heightened awareness of the prevalence of this "victim as criminal" attitude. When the California decision was handed down organizers were able to mobilize large numbers of people quickly. Three hundred demonstrators picketed the California Court of Appeals to manifest their displeasure.

The criterion for the success of protest movements of this kind is whether it activates third parties, especially the media and the liberal community, in ways favorable to protest goals.(21) The powerlessness of women, so well exemplified in the wife abuse and rape victim cases, can be reduced to the extent that third parties intervene to demand active police prosecution of husbands who beat their wives or resignation of judges who view rape differently from other crimes of violence. Protest actions succeed if they stimulate this third-party intervention.

The weakness of this protest model, most fully developed in the "politics of poor people" literature(22) is that the compromising necessary in order to bring these newly acquired third-party resources to bear fully, may undercut the support of the powerless for the protest organization. The case of the NOW organization in Onega, where the Commission on the Status of Women was studied in depth, illustrates this point.

From its inception until about 1976 Onega NOW had functioned largely as a protest group. But by 1976 the leader of the NOW group came to feel strongly that many of the organization's protest objectives could be served most effectively by closer cooperation with the Commission on the Status of Women. Acting on this belief she accepted an appointment on the commission and proceeded to join NOW and the CSW in co-sponsoring a Women's Equality Day celebration. The NOW membership included a substantial lesbian component, so much so that the chairperson reported: "To be truthful I think Onega sees the whole NOW group as gay." But the gay/straight difference had never caused dissension in the organization. As co-sponsors of the Women's Equality Day event, NOW members naturally wanted to help shape the panels. They suggested topics to the NOW chair - by then also involved with the commission - recommending panels on lesbian mothers, lesbian women, etc. After meeting with the commission chair the NOW leader recognized that including such topics was simply not politically feasible. She explained to the NOW membership: "I think that's a little too much. If it was a NOW conference I could see it. But you are going to have the Junior League there, the AAUW. They're not going to go with it. . . . I'm really sorry, but that's just the way it's going to have to be."

The lesbian NOW members deeply resented what they perceived as an unacceptable compromise of principle engaged in by their chairperson. Clearly their support for the NOW organization as such waned, although it is still too early to judge the long-term implications of these events. Still the case does illustrate the general point that fully utilizing third-party support which a protest group might generate may jeopardize the support of the membership of the protest organization.

BUREAUCRATIC POLITICS: PROGRAMS THAT SUCCEED

Change by means of bureaucratic organization represents a third model for advancing women's movement objectives. The assumption here is that change can only be securely effected through a bureaucratic process. Thus government administrative officials implement changes, many of which they themselves have initiated through their inherent agenda shaping role.

At the national level the Women's Bureau in the United States Department of Labor springs to mind immediately as illustrating this model of change. Some state governments have also institutionalized a women's bureau counterpart in the states, generally labeled women's divisions. Recently in community political systems we have seen a burgeoning of organizations premised on this change by bureaucracy rationale. Generally their purposes are not directed strictly to helping the powerless, as are protest organizations. Nor are they particularly concerned with the process aspects of their activity, as are the Commissions on the Status of Women. Rather their focus is programmatic, and their concern is with impact. Fair employment practice boards (dealing with sex discrimination) and women's centers, as administrative components of local governments, illustrate this type of change effort.

The fair employment practice board is a still rare but growing component of county and city governments across the United States. Charged with investigating and, in some communities, hearing complaints of sex and race discrimination, this organization consists of a citizen board and an executive director who manages an investigative staff. The role of the board is to hear cases appealed from the administrative decision of the executive director. However, the staff, under the guidance of the executive director, investigates charges of discrimination, reports findings and the director then renders an administrative judgment as to the compensation that is in order. Success is measured directly by the number of complaints successfully resolved.

The women's center, also still rare as a component of local government, exists to provide both a setting and the oversight necessary to effect a broad range of services available to women in a community. Specific program activities would include workshops on divorce and custody, investment and estate planning, and career development and employment. A center might also operate a number of counseling and support activities on topics ranging from "single awareness," to "postmastectomy," to "nutritional awareness." Such centers are staffed with trained counselors. Evaluation is keyed to the meeting of individual women's needs and success is measured by the numbers of women participating in the programs and the satisfaction that participants report.

The peculiar advantage of the bureaucratic model, as reflected in both examples, is that it provides both the authority structure and the resources necessary to produce strong results - oriented programmatic responses to women's policy problems. Reflecting on the local CSW, the head of a department of human relations in Onega noted, "Policy is made on the executive level of government [thus] . . . advisory groups [like the CSW] play a very very small role; and they're wasting their time if that's what they are really trying to get done, to make policy." The bureaucratic model would direct activist resources toward institutionalizing the women's movement inside the executive branch so as to insure that positive change objectives are not ignored in policy making.

The bureaucratic model also has a negative side. One activist, interviewed in the course of the commission study, put her misgivings about change through bureaucracy in this way: "When you're organizing around political issues and you've got a bureaucratic government agency to go through, it slows you down alot . . . worrying about which level you can go to, what the protocol is, that kind of thing. . . ." Another activist leader, reflecting specifically on the pitfalls of a governmentally funded women's center in her own community, suggested that co-optation by the county government was almost inevitable. The co-optation comes, in her view, through the desire of organizations to grow: "It [the women's center] becomes a vested interest. When you are competing for money you have to produce, and in order to produce, you have to have things on paper - things to show, and it gets out of hand."

Few advocates of the bureaucratic change model would deny that working within government imposes constraints on activities and creates potentially threatening incentives for organizational conservatism. However, they respond to this critical line of argument by asserting that the bureaucratic official is best located to initiate and implement change, and that some change, measured in terms of real impact, is worth more than the most noble unfulfilled objectives.

ACTIVIST RESOURCES:
WHERE SHOULD THEY CONCENTRATE?

Given these alternative models for organizing activist efforts behind change in the condition of women at the community level, how might we answer the question posed in the beginning chapter of this study: Do Commissions on the Status of Women merit the substantial commitment of activist resources they command?

In fairness the Commissions on the Status of Women can be assessed only in terms of the pluralist model within which they operate. The earlier analysis outlined the kinds of activities and issues occupying a set of five particularly successful commissions (chapter 3). Later chapters assessed these five commissions in terms of their agenda-building capability (chapter 4) and their capacity to satisfy various audiences (chapter 5). This analysis reached the conclusion that while certain contextual variables seem associated with a commission's propensity to deal with certain constellations of issues, and to please certain audiences, some issues and audiences remain ignored. For example, neither the unequal justice for welfare mothers issue nor the lesbian audience seems likely to occupy much commission time or energy in the five successful commissions analyzed. To actively pursue either this issue or this audience would dramatically decrease the commission's capacity to remain successful in the pluralist politics framework.

Still one can raise the question: Should activists commit their resources to any institution that operates on the basis of the pluralist model? Does pluralist politics by its very nature channel issues and interest so as to retard genuine social change? One answer to this question asserts: it can, but it is

not predestined to do so.   The key to understanding whether
or not commitment of activist resources to a pluralist institution is appropriate resides in particular characteristics of the
individual community.   The base points of the radical and the
conservative differ by community, and thus the political
context necessarily shapes the constellation of values the CSW
can comfortably represent.   The commissions are institutions
designed to represent the modal women's movement thinking in
the community - not either extreme.   We know that whatever
else organizations seek, they seek to survive.(23)   And for
Commissions on the Status of Women survival means staying in
touch with this modal force.   Commissions on the Status of
Women can play a critical role in legitimizing that modal
interest.   Rather than faulting the CSWs for being the
pluralist institutions that they are, we should acknowledge that
activists have multiple roles to play in advancing change at the
community level.
      Viewing the advancement of positive change in develop-
mental terms, where models of organization and politics fit
with particular phases in policy development provides a
framework for acknowledging the unique contribution of each
organizational form.   Figure 6.1 exhibits the types of politics
through which interests manifest themselves in the process of
attaining improved conditions for women in the community.

Protest	Pluralist	Bureaucratic
Politics	Politics	Politics

Fig. 6.1.   Types of politics and their interrelationship.

      Protest politics is not only desirable but may be essential
for powerless people to create political resources.   While many
recent changes in the condition of women have proven favorable to women as a class, all women have not benefited
equally.   Pockets of startling female powerlessness mark the
community terrain.   The change interests of many powerless
women will be secured only when they gain the attention of
certain community elites.   Protest action serves that goal.
      The pluralist politics phase takes over once demands for
change come to be viewed as at least minimally legitimate,
and here the Commission on the Status of Women can play a
critical role.   Working with both old but unfulfilled and newly
legitimized demands for change, the commission can channel
mainstream activist resources toward central pressure points in
the local policy-making system.   All the commission activities
(chapter 3) come into play in this effort.

Still in many areas, where public policy touches the lives of women, change can be best guaranteed if responsibility is placed in a government agency. The bureaucracy model ties both resources and professional careers to promoting change from within; thus bureaucratic politics emerges as third stage in producing social and political change.

Reflecting back on the case raised in the Onega community, where the two welfare mothers were charged with manslaughter rather than neglect, provides an occasion for illustrating these developmental stages. In that tragedy the leadership of the welfare mothers organization, together with feminist-welfare rights lawyers might have formed a defense committee. Immediately the committee could publicize the inequity of the charge and organize a demonstration at the first judicial hearing in order to secure a reduction of charges and to make known both the lack of support for welfare mothers and the unequal justice they receive. Protest at this stage of this issue is the appropriate form for commitment of activist resources. At a later stage, with some degree of public support for women in such circumstances clearly in evidence, the Commission on the Status of Women could appoint an ad hoc committee to study and recommend steps the local governing officials might take to reduce the likelihood of such an occurrence again: more day-care services, city-sponsored parent-support systems, training sessions to sensitize police to racism and sexism in charging people with crimes. Finally some of these recommendations to be effectively implemented must become institutionalized: a women's division of legal aid, the establishment of a women's center where support services could be provided or arranged, etc.

Yet it may be that the very institutions charged with bringing to fruition change objectives, say a women's center in this case, could fall victim to an organizational conservatism which would stimulate renewed protest action on the part of powerless women. As the arrow on figure 6.1 connecting bureaucratic politics to protest politics implies, the interests of the powerless can ultimately be jeopardized by the very institutions inaugurated to advance them. In other words, the normal practices of bureaucratic politics may spark a renewed protest action.

Obviously all interests do not proceed lockstep to fulfillment through each of these political-organizational forms. But each form, each type of politics, does play a critical role in realizing some interests, at some time. Thus the question, Should we commit women's movement resources to Commissions on the Status of Women? elicits a strong positive response in settings where the community perceives at least some women's movement change demands as legitimate.

FUTURE RESEARCH AGENDA

This analysis of alternative change models, concluding by acknowledging the inherent values of each form suggests two areas for future research in the study of women in community politics. First we need to explore in greater depth the strengths and limits of protest, bureaucratic, and pluralist institutions at the various stages marking the development of women's concerns in community politics. Second, we must explore ways in which organizations premised on different models of change can work together more effectively. Clearly a condition of keen competition among leaders in each type of organization militates against achieving shared long range objectives.

The ultimate criteria for assessing any political organization is the extent to which it makes the governors more responsible to the governed,(24) while integrating the governed into the decision-making process.(25) Commissions on the Status of Women and other women's movement institutions will be held, in the final analysis, to this standard. This proposed direction for future research promises to yield information which both facilitates holding women's movement institutions to a meaningful accountability and offers direction to those institutions for more fully meeting their charge.

Appendix A —
Interview Schedule

1. Structure

Ask Executive
Director: (1a.)   Authorizing Enactment

                    (1b.)   Size Commission

                            Staff

                    (1c.)   Location in Governmental Structure

                    (1d.)   Appointment Procedure
                            Commission

                            Staff

                    (1e.)   Task Sub-Structure

2. Resources

Ask Executive
Director: (2a.)   Budget
                            Appropriations <u>73-74</u>   <u>74-75</u>   <u>75-76</u>   <u>76-77</u>

                            Grants

                            Other Sources

                    (2b.)   Could you describe the procedure
                            involved in your budget request
                            approval?

                    (2c.)   Do Commission members receive
                            compensation for out of pocket
                            expenses?
                            _____Yes   _____No   _____Sometimes

117

(2d.) What percentage of Commission funding is designated for staff support?

(3a.)
Ask All:

How would you characterize the role of the executive director?

(3b.)
Ask Executive
Director/CSW
Members:

How would you describe the role played by the executive director vis-a-vis the commissioners?

(3c.)
Ask Executive
Director/CSW
Members/Local
Elected Officials:

How would you characterize the role played by the executive director vis-a-vis the local legislative body?

(3d.)
Ask Executive
Director/CSW
Members/Local
Administrative
Officials:

How would you characterize the role played by the executive director vis-a-vis the local administrator (manager; Human Relations Commission Director; Affirmative Action Officer, etc.)?

(3e.)
Ask All:

How would you characterize the role of the commission members?

(3f.)
Ask Executive
Director/CSW
Members/Local
Elected Officials:

Do Commission members have contact with elected officials: About how often? Could you give some examples?

(3g.)
Ask Executive
Director/CSW
Members/Local
Administrators:

Do Commission members have contact with local administrators? About how often? Could you give some examples?

4.
Ask Local
Officials/
Administrators
CSW Members/
Executive Director: In terms of initiating activities and
                          deciding how to pursue them, do you
                          believe that decision making should be in
                          the hands of the Commission, the staff, or
                          shared equally by Commission and staff?

5.
Ask All (If
Center exists):   How do you see the Women's Center
                          fitting into the picture of CSW activity?
                          As an integral part of CSW, primarily a
                          staff function with some CSW support, or
                          exclusively a staff function?

6.   Functions, Strategies and Issues

Ask All: What do you see as the major goals of a
                          CSW in _____?

7.
Ask All: I have completed a list of goal areas for
                          commissions on women. This list is drawn
                          from examination of a large number of
                          Commission reports. (Hand card with
                          goal areas list) How important would you
                          say each goal area is using this scale?
                          (Hand card with importance scale)

8.
Ask All: Now, using this scale, how effective do
                          you feel the Commission has been over
                          the past year, in each of these areas?
                          (Hand card with effectiveness scale)

9.
Ask Executive
Director/CSW
Members: Which strategies have you found to be
                          most effective in each of these goal areas?
                          Which strategies have you found to be
                          least effective?

10.   Activities/Programs

(10a.)
Ask Executive
Director/CSW
Members: In which of the following substantive
                          areas has your Commission been active?

Major activity is defined as the work of a
committee or task force, while minor
activity involves such activity as letter
writing. (Hand card with substantive
activity area list) Now, using this scale,
how important would you say each activity
area has been to the Commission over the
past year. (Hand card with importance
scale)

GOAL AREAS	IMPORTANCE SCALE

Public Education/Consciousness Raising	5 of absolutely top importance
Needs Assessment	4 of great importance
"Watchdog"/Investigation	3 of moderate importance
Expansion of Political Participation/Women	2 of little importance
Direct Influence in Local/ State/Federal Policy Making	1 of no importance
Convener/Catalyst	0 don't know/can't say
Direct Support Service	

(10b.)
Ask Executive
Director/CSW
Members:

Next, how effective would you say the
Commission has been in each of the areas
over the past year? (Hand card with
effectiveness scale)

EFFECTIVENESS SCALE
5 Completely Effective
4 Very Effective
3 Moderately Effective
2 Slightly Effective
1 Not Effective
0 Don't know/Can't Say

(10c.)
Ask Elected
Officials/
Administrators/
Women's Group
Leaders: Here is a list of substantive issue areas
                         which might be of special concern to
                         women. (Hand card with substantive
                         activity area list) Using this scale, how
                         important would you say each of these
                         issues is in your county/city? (Hand
                         card with importance scale)

SUBSTANTIVE ISSUE AREAS   IMPORTANCE SCALE

SUBSTANTIVE ISSUE AREAS	IMPORTANCE SCALE
Education and Training	5 of absolutely top importance
Employment	
Child Care	4 of great importance
Health Care	
Political Participation	3 of moderate importance
of Women	
Credit	2 of little importance
Insurance	
Tax Law	1 of no importance
Housing	
Rape	0 don't know/can't say
ERA	
Family Planning	
Female Offenders	
Abortion	
Sexual Preference	
Battered Women	
Self-Assertiveness/	
Psychology of Women	
Consciousness Raising	
on Media	
Ethnic Minority Issues	
Legal Rights in Marriage	
and Family	
Other	

(10d.)
Ask Elected
Officials/
Administrators/
Women's Group
Leaders:

Next, how effective would you say the Commission on Women has been in each of these issue areas? (Hand card with effectiveness scale)

EFFECTIVENESS SCALE

---

5 Completely Effective

4 Very Effective

3 Moderately Effective

2 Slightly Effective

1 Not Effective

0 Don't Know/Can't Say

11.
Ask All: What are the major obstacles to increased effectiveness of the CSW generally?

12.
Ask All: How would you measure the CSW's effectiveness? What would you look at? (Indicators)

13.
Ask All: How would you describe the constituency of the CSW?

14.
Ask All: Who, in your view, benefits most from CSW activities?

15.
Ask All: What would you say are the 4 or 5 most visible women's organizations (not necessarily feminist) in _____?

16.
Ask All: What are the 4 or 5 influential (in policy impact sense) women's organizations (not necessarily feminist) in _____?

17.
Ask All: What are the most visible feminist organi-
                             zations?

18.
Ask All: What are the most influential (in a policy
                             impact sense) feminist organizations?

19.
Ask Executive
Director/CSW
Members: Now I will name a number of women's
                             organizations in this community.   As I
                             name them, I would like you to character-
                             ize the quality of the Commission's work-
                             ing relationship with each organization,
                             using the scale.   (Hand card with rela-
                             tionship scale)

QUALITY OF RELATIONSHIP SCALE

---

5 Excellent working relationship

4 Good working relationship

3 Fair working relationship

2 Poor working relationship

1 No working relationship

0 Can't say/Don't know

20.
Ask Executive
Director/CSW
Members: How would you describe your interaction
                             with:

                             (20a.) State CSW
                             (20b.) Other Local CSW?
                             (20c.) National Association CSW?
                             (20d.) Women's Bureau?

21.   Committee Information

Ask CSW Committee Chair-
persons: SUBJECT _____

                    SIZE _____

                    BUDGET _____

(21a.) How would you describe the leadership structure of your task force? How did you become chairperson and how do you see that role?

(21b.) How do you staff your task force? How do you use non-commission members? What do you look for in selecting them?

(21c.) How much time, per month, do you regularly spend on task force work?

(21d.) Do you try to secure a time commitment from potential task force members?

(21e.) How often do you meet formally as a task force?

(21f.) Do you encourage non-task force members to attend?

(21g.) What have been the major concerns of your task force over the past year?

(21h.) What did or do you expect to achieve as an outcome of these efforts?

(21i.) Which groups have you found most useful in supporting the achievement of your objectives?

(21j.) How would you measure the effectiveness of your task force? What would you look at?

22. Personal Agenda
Ask All: Now I would like to ask you a question about your own views on the needs of women in _____ . Putting aside for a moment the question of whether a particular need area can or should be met by a CSW, how would you describe your own personal agenda for women in _____ . What problem area are most pressing for women?

Appendix B —
Personal Profile
Questionnaire

The following information is CONFIDENTIAL. It will not be used for individual identification. Its purpose is to provide a basis for aggregate description of local Commissions on Women.

Respondent Code Number _____

Date of Birth _____

Marital Status _____

Occupation and Job Title _____

Spouse's Occupation _____

Religious Preference _____

Race _____

Please circle the last year of formal education you completed:

       Grade School: 1st 2nd 3rd 4th 5th 6th 7th 8th
        High School: 9th 10th 11th 12th
            College: Freshman Sophomore Junior Senior
       Graduate or Professional: 1 2 3 4 5 6 7 8 9 10
       Other (Please specify) _____

Annual Family Income, before taxes:

    ( ) under $4,000
    ( ) 4,000 - 7,999
    ( ) 8,000 - 11,999
    ( ) 12,000 - 13,999
    ( ) 14,000 - 15,999
    ( ) 16,000 - 19,999
    ( ) 20,000 - 29,999
    ( ) 30,000 and over

Do you mainly consider yourself a

    ( ) Democrat
    ( ) Republican
    ( ) Other _____

Have you ever run for elected public office?

    ( ) yes
    ( ) no

Do you intend to run for elected public office within the next three or four years?

    ( ) yes
    ( ) no

How would you describe yourself in terms of community involvement?

very involved   not at all involved
   10   9   8   7   6   5   4   3   2   1   0

_____

How would you describe yourself in terms of political participation?

very active   no activity
   10   9   8   7   6   5   4   3   2   1   0

_____

How would you describe yourself in terms of involvement in the women's movement?

very involved   not at all involved
     10   9   8   7   6   5   4   3   2   1   0

Please list the specific organizations (women's organizations, civic groups, unions, political organizations, professional associations, etc.) in which you are most active.

Notes

CHAPTER 1

(1) See especially Jo Freeman, The Politics of Women's Liberation: A Case Study of an Emerging Social Movement and Its Relation to the Policy Process (New York: David McKay Co., 1975).

(2) See for example Irene Diamond, Sex Roles in the State House (New Haven: Yale University Press, 1977); Jeanne Kirkpatrick, Political Woman (New York: Basic Books, 1974); or Rita Mae Kelly and Mary Boutilier, The Making of Political Woman (Chicago: Nelson-Hall, 1978).

(3) Sidney Verba, "Democratic Participation," Annals of the American Academy of Political and Social Science, vol. 2, Social Goals and Indicators for American Society 373 (September 1967): 54.

(4) Ibid., p. 55.

(5) For a discussion of types of representation, see Hanna Pitkin, The Concept of Representation (Berkeley: University of California Press, 1967), pp. 60-143.

(6) Thomas R. Wolanin, Presidential Advisory Commissions: Truman to Nixon (Madison: University of Wisconsin Press, 1975), p. 80.

(7) David Truman, The Governmental Process (New York: Alfred A. Knopf, 1951), p. 458.

(8) "'Cheap' Brainpower in Washington - Boon or Boondoggle," U.S. News and World Report, March 1976, p. 63.

(9) Alan L. Dean, "Ad Hoc Commissions for Policy Formation?" in The Presidential Advisory System, ed. Thomas E. Cronin and Sanford D. Greenberg (New York: Harper and Row, 1969), pp. 106-110.

(10)   Personal interview with Jane Patterson (civil rights activist), Greensboro, N.C., December 1976.
(11)   Martin Gruberg, "Official Commissions on the Status of Women: A Worldwide Movement" (Paper delivered at the Annual Meeting of the American Political Science Association, New Orleans, La., September 4-8, 1973), p. 15.
(12)   Gruberg, "Official Commissions," p. 3; and U.S. Department of Labor, Women's Bureau, International Division, "A Listing of United Nations Meetings, 1962-78 That Have Given Special Attention to the Need for National Machinery Such as Bureaus and Commissions," mimeographed.
(13)   Gruberg, "Official Commissions," p. 58.
(14)   Judith Hole and Ellen Levine, Rebirth of Feminism (New York: Quadrangle Books, 1971), p. 18.
(15)   Ibid., p. 20.
(16)   Interview with Edward Bershtein, Staff Liaison for Representative Edith Green, Madison, Wis., July 29, 1977.
(17)   Hole and Levine, Rebirth, p. 19.
(18)   Ibid., p. 24.
(19)   New York Times, August 1, 1965, p. 6.
(20)   Ellen Boneparth, "The Impact of Commissions on the Status of Women on the Policy of Making Process: A California Case Study" (Paper presented at the Annual Meeting of the American Political Science Association, Chicago, September 2-5, 1976.
(21)   U.S. Department of Labor, Women's Bureau, Employment Standards Administration, "A Compilation of Data on State and Local Commissions on Women," mimeographed, 1973, 1975.
(22)   Albert K. Karnig and B. Olive Walter, "Election of Women to City Councils," Social Science Quarterly 56 (March 1976): 605-13.
(23)   Marilyn Falik, "Comment on Ideology and Theory: Pre-Methodological Issues," The Study of Women and Politics: A Symposium Exploring Methodological Issues, ed. Sarah Schramm (forthcoming), p. 16.
(24)   See John A. Williams, "Political Leadership and Governmental Performance," Comparative Studies Association, Comparative Interdisciplinary Section, Working Paper no. 65 (April 1976).
(25)   Rita Mae Kelly and Mary Boutilier, "The Self-Fulfilling Prophecy and the Study of Political Women," in The Study of Women and Politics: A Symposium Exploring Methodological Issues, ed. Sarah Schramm (forthcoming).
(26)   Ibid.
(27)   Melissa A. Butler, "Ideology and Methodology in the Study of Images of Women in Political Thought" (Con-

ference paper delivered at the Annual Meeting of the
Southern Political Science Association, Atlanta, Ga.,
November 3-5, 1976, p. 4.

(28) For a comprehensive review of the literature, see John
D. Hutcheson, Jr., and Jann Shevin, Citizen Groups in
Local Politics: A Bibliographic Review (Santa Barbara,
Calif.: Cleo Books, 1976).

(29) For an example of this type of work and a source for
reference to similar research, see Jean J. Kirkpatrick,
Political Women (New York: Basic Books, 1974).

(30) For a presentation of this perspective, see Peter
Bachrach, The Theory of Democratic Elitism: A Critique
(Boston: Little, Brown and Co., 1976). For a more
recent work summarizing the concept of participation in a
broader context, see Jerrold G. Rush, "Political Participation in America: A Review Essay," American Political
Science Review 70 (June 1976): 583-91.

CHAPTER 2

(1) See John A. Williams, "Political Leadership and Governmental Performance," Comparative Studies Association,
Comparative Interdisciplinary Section, Working Paper no.
65 (April 1976).

(2) Ibid., p. 7.

(3) Ibid.

(4) For a discussion of goal areas as areas of operating
activity, see the model of organizational effectiveness
in Amitai Etzioni, A Comparative Analysis of Complex Organizations (New York: Free Press, 1975), pp. 136-37.

(5) Information acquired from a survey conducted by the
U.S. Department of Labor, Women's Bureau, Employment
Standards Administration, 1975.

(6) Robert C. Fried, "Comparative Urban Research," University of California at Los Angeles, European Urban
Research, Working Paper no. 1 (reissued September
1973), p. 32. It should be noted that "urban" is often
used interchangeably with "community" to characterize a
substantial body of research which employs a comparative
method to focus on local political systems. One edited
collection containing some of the classic research in this
area illustrates the point. The collection is entitled State
and Urban Politics, but the table of contents designates
the local focus as "community" political systems rather
than "urban" political systems, and the word urban
occurs only once in an individually titled contribution.
See Richard I. Hofferbert and Ira Sharkansky, State and
Urban Politics (Boston: Little, Brown and Co., 1971).

(7)   Operational measures and the supporting literature for variables that require elucidation are as follows: 1) political culture (commission communities are coded on a 1-to-6 scale with 1 = moralistic, 2 = predominantly moralistic, 3 = somewhat moralistic, 4 = individualistic, 5 = predominant or somewhat individualistic, and 6 = traditional) see Daniel Elazer, American Federalism: A View From the States, 2nd ed. (New York: Thomas Y. Crowell Co., 1972), pp. 106-107; 2) citizen participation (5 adults with 4 years of high school), see Michael Aiken and Robert R. Alford, "Community Structure and Innovation: The Case of Public Housing," American Political Science Review 64 (September 1970): 843-64; 3) reform (percentage nonpartisan), see Michael Aiken and Robert R. Alford, "Community Structure and Innovation: The Case of Urban Renewal," American Sociological Review 35 (August 1970): 650-65; 4) public regard (percentage foreign stock in population and percentage children in private elementary and high school), see Edward C. Banfield and James Q. Wilson, City Politics (Cambridge, Mass.: Harvard University Press, 1963); 5) form of election (percentage exclusively at large), see Aiken and Alford, "The Case of Urban Renewal," pp. 650-65; 6) jurisdiction (percentage city); 7) concentration of community power (percentage of managers, proprietors, and officials reported in U.S. Census), see Amos Hawley, "Community Power Structure and Urban Renewal Success," American Journal of Sociology 68 (January 1963): 422-31; 8) community integration (percentage unemployed in labor force), see Maurice Pinard, "Structural Attachments and Political Support in Urban Politics: The Case of Fluoridation Referendums," American Journal of Sociology 68 (March 1963): 513-26; and 9) poverty (percentage of families below poverty level), see Aiken and Alford, "The Case of Urban Renewal," pp. 650-65.

(8)   See Aiken and Alford, "The Case of Urban Renewal," pp. 650-65; see also Aiken and Alford, "The Case of Public Housing," pp. 843-64.

(9)   See Aiken and Alford, "The Case of Urban Renewal," pp. 650-65; see also Hawley, "Community Power Structure," 422-31.

CHAPTER 3

(1)   Lawrence B. Mohr, "The Concept of Organizational Goal," American Political Science Review 58 (June 1973): 470.

(2)   Jeanne Nicholson, "Perceptions of Organizational Goals and Effectiveness: A Study of Four Metropolitan Washington Women's Commission" (Ph.D. diss., Department of Political Science, Johns Hopkins University, 1976), p. 225.

(3)   Amitai Etzioni, Modern Organizations (Englewood Cliffs, N. J.: Prentice-Hall, 1964), p. 6.

(4)   For this distinction between goal components, see Nicholson, "Perceptions of Organizational Goals," p. 225.

(5)   Ibid., p. 265.

(6)   Daniel Bell, "Government by Commission," in The Presidential Advisory System, ed. Thomas Cronin and Sanford Greenberg (New York: Harper and Row, 1969).

(7)   U.S. Department of Labor, Handbook for Commissions on the Status of Women, A report prepared in cooperation with the Women's Bureau, Employment Standards Administration, (Madison; University of Wisconsin, 1974).

(8)   Naomi Lynn, "Women in American Politics: An Overview," Women: A Feminist Perspective, ed. Jo. Freeman (Palo Alto, Calif.: Mayfield Publishing Co., 1975), p. 374.

(9)   "U.S. National Women's Agenda," Social Policy, 6 (March/April 1976): 24-25.

(10) See Joyce M. Mitchell and William C. Mitchell, Political Analysis and Public Policy (Chicago: Rand McNally and Co., 1969), p. 147; and Elizabeth Drew, "On Giving Oneself a Hotfoot: Government by Commission," Atlantic Monthly 221 (May 1968): 45-49.

(11) See Drew, "Government by Commission," pp. 45-49; and George T. Sulzner, "The Policy Process and the Uses of National Government Commissions," Western Political Quarterly 30 (September 1971): 438-48.

(12) Roger W. Cobb and Charles D. Elder, Participation in American Politics: The Dynamics of Agenda-Building (Baltimore: Johns Hopkins Press, 1975).

(13) The recent literature developing this thesis is rooted in an earlier article by Ronald Inglehart, "The Silent Revolution in Europe: Intergovernmental Change in Post-Industrial Societies," American Political Science Review 65 (December 1971): 991-1017. See also Debra Stewart, "Taxeconomic Development in Women's Policy Studies: A Proposed Direction" (Manuscript, Department of Political Science, North Carolina State University, 1977).

(14) For a discussion of data suggesting restrictive policies and inequitable distribution of services prior to the June 1977 Supreme Court decisions, see Richard Lincoln et al., "The Court, the Congress and the President: Turning Back the Clock on the Pregnant Poor," Family Planning Perspectives 9 (September/October 1977): 210-11.

CHAPTER 4

(1) Roger W. Cobb and Charles D. Elder, Participation in American Politics: The Dynamics of Agenda-Building (Baltimore: Johns Hopkins Press, 1975), p. 16.
(2) For a discussion of the potential symbolic rewards, see Murray Edelman, The Symbolic Use of Politics (Urbana: University of Illinois Press, 1967); see also Murray Edelman, Politics as Symbolic Action: Mass Arousal and Quiescence (Chicago: Academy Press, 1971).
(3) Cobb and Elder, Dynamics of Agenda-Building, p. 10.
(4) Ibid., p. 14.
(5) Ibid., p. 82.
(6) Debra Stewart, "Taxeconomic Development in Women's Policy Studies: A Proposed Direction" (Manuscript, Department of Political Science, North Carolina State University, 1977), p. 3.
(7) L. Harmon Ziegler and G. Wayne Peak, Interest Groups in American Society (Englewood Cliffs, N. J.: Prentice-Hall, 1972), p. 3.
(8) For a distinction between terms developed, see A. Paul Pross, ed., Pressure Group Behavior in Canadian Politics (Scarborough, Ontario: McGraw-Hill Ryerson, 1975), p. 2.
(9) Jo Freeman, The Politics of Women's Liberation: A Case Study of an Emerging Social Movement and its Relation to the Policy Process (New York: David McKay Co., 1975), pp. 71-72.
(10) Frank X. Steggert, Community Action Groups and City Government: Perspectives from Ten American Cities (Cambridge, Mass.: Ballinger Publishing Co., 1975), p. 28.
(11) James Q. Wilson, Political Organizations (New York: Basic Books, 1973), p. 221.
(12) Del Martin and Phyllis Lyon, Lesbian/Women (San Francisco: Glide Publications, 1972), p. 7.
(13) For a summary of this literature, see Wilson, Political Organizations, p. 10 ff.

CHAPTER 5

(1) For a well-developed discussion of the distinction between "client" and "constituency," see Eugene Lewis, American Politics in a Bureaucratic Age: Citizens, Constituents, Clients and Victims (Cambridge, Mass.: Winthrop Publishers, 1977), pp. 10-20.

(2)   See Richard H. Hall, Organizations: Structure and
      Process (Englewood Cliffs, N. J.: Prentice-Hall, 1972);
      and Ephraim Yuchtman and Stanley E. Seashore, "System
      Resource   Approach   to   Organizational   Effectiveness,"
      American Sociological Review 32 (December 1967): 891-903.
(3)   See Charles Perrow, "The Analysis of Goals in Complex
      Organizations," American Sociological Review 26 (December
      1961):   854-66;   B.   S.   Georgopoulos and Arnold S.
      Tannebaum, "A Study of Organizational Effectiveness,"
      American Sociological Review 22 (October 1957), 534-50;
      and Paul E. Mott, The Characteristics of Effective
      Organizations (New York: Harper and Row, 1972). For
      an empirical comparison of these two approaches, see
      Joseph J. Molnar and David L. Rogers, "Organizational
      Effectiveness: An Empirical Comparison of the Goal and
      System Resource Approaches," Sociological Quarterly 17
      (Summer 1976), 401-13.
(4)   For a general discussion of problems encountered in
      empirically identifying goals, see James Price, "The Study
      of Organizational Effectiveness," Sociological Quarterly 13
      (Winter 1972): 12.
(5)   B. S. Georgopoulos and Floyd C. Mann, The Community
      General Hospital (New York: Macmillan Co., 1962).
(6)   Lewis, American Politics, p. 10.
(7)   Frank X. Steggert, Community Action Groups and City
      Government: Perspectives from Ten American Cities
      (Cambridge, Mass.: Ballinger Publishing Co., 1975), p.
      61.
(8)   For a discussion of this distinction, see Judith Hole and
      Ellen Levine, Rebirth of Feminism (New York: Quad-
      rangle Books, 1971); and Maren Carden Lockwood, The
      New Feminist Movement (New York: Russell Sage Founda-
      tion, 1974).
(9)   Jo Freeman, The Politics of Women's Liberation   (New
      York: David McKay Co., 1975).
(10) Graham T. Allison, Essence of Decision (Boston: Little,
      Brown and Co., 1971), p. 176.

CHAPTER 6

(1)   Kenneth M. Dolbeare, Political Change in the United
      States: A Framework for Analysis (New York: McGraw-
      Hill, 1974), p. 8.
(2)   Thomas R. Dye and L. Harmon Zeigler, The Irony of
      Democracy (Belmont, Calif.: Duxbury Press, 1971), p.
      14.
(3)   This summary is based on the discussion of pluralism in
      Thomas R. Dye, Politics in States and Communities, 3rd

ed. (Englewood Cliffs, N. J.:   Prentice-Hall, 1977), pp. 338-55.

(4)   See, Dolbeare, Political Change; Theodore J. Lowi, The Politics of Disorder (New York: Basic Books, 1971); and Frances Fox Piven and Richard A. Cloward, Poor People's Movements: Why They Succeed and How They Fail (New York: Pantheon, 1978).

(5)   Michael Lipsky, "Protest as a Political Resource," American Political Science Review 62 (December 1968): 1145.

(6)   James Q. Wilson, Political Organizations (New York: Basic Books, 1973), p. 282.

(7)   Ibid.

(8)   Eugene Lewis, American Politics in a Bureaucratic Age: Citizens, Constituents, Clients and Victims (Cambridge, Mass.: Winthrop Publishers, 1977), chap. 1.

(9)   This summary is based on the discussion of bureaucracy in Lewis, American Politics, pp. 169-70.

(10) Saul D. Alinsky, Rules for Radicals: A Practical Primer for Realistic Radicals (New York: Random House, 1971), p. 113.

(11) Ehud Harari, "Japanese Politics: Advice in Comparative Perspective," Public Policy 20 (Fall 1974).

(12) Ibid., 539.

(13) Margaret Mead and Frances Balgley Kaplan, eds., American Woman: Report of the President's Commission on the Status of Women and Other Publications of the Commission (New York: Charles Scribner's Sons, 1965), p. 16.

(14) Ibid., 207-209, Executive Order 10980.

(15) E. E. Schattschneider, The Semisovereign People (New York: Holt, Rinehart, and Winston, 1960), p. 35.

(16) Alinsky, Rules for Radicals.

(17) Piven and Cloward, Poor People's Movements.

(18) Judith Nole and Ellen Levine, Rebirth of Feminism (New York: Quadrangle Books, 1971), p. 123.

(19) Ibid., p. 124.

(20) For elaboration see, ibid., pp. 125-35.

(21) Lipsky, "Protest as a Political Resource," p. 1153.

(22) See Piven and Cloward, Poor People's Movement.

(23) Wilson, Political Organizations, p. 10.

(24) Heintz Eulau and Kenneth Prewitt, Labyrinths of Democracy (Indianapolis: Bobbs-Merrill, 1973), p. 24.

(25) Peter Bachrach, The Theory of Democratic Elitism (Boston: Little, Brown and Co., 1967).

Bibliography

Adams, J. Stacy. Interviewing Procedures. Chapel Hill: University of North Carolina Press, 1958.

Aiken, Michael, and Alford, Robert R. "Community Structure and Innovation: The Case of Urban Renewal." American Sociological Review 35 (August 1970): 650-65.

_____. "Community Structure and Innovation: The Case of Public Housing." American Political Science Review. 64 (September 1970): 843-64.

Akins, Carl. "The Riot Commission Report and the Notion of Political Truth". Social Science Quarterly 49 (December 1968): 469-73.

Alinsky, Saul D. Rules for Radicals: A Practical Primer for Realistic Radicals. New York: Random House, 1971.

Allison, Graham T. Essence of Decision. Boston: Little, Brown and Co., 1971.

Bachrach, Peter. The Theory of Democratic Elitism: A Critique. Boston: Little, Brown and Co., 1971.

Bales, Robert F. "Task Roles and Social Roles in Problem-Solving Groups." In Readings in Social Psychology, edited by Eleanor F. Maccoby, Theodore M. Newcomb, and Eugene L. Harley. New York: Henry Holt, 1958.

Banfield, Edward C., and Wilson, James Q. City Politics. Cambridge, Mass.: Harvard University Press, 1963.

Bell, Daniel. "Government by Commission." In The Presidential Advisory System, edited by Thomas Cronin and Sanford Greenberg. New York: Harper and Row, 1969.

Boneparth, Ellen. "The Impact of Commissions on the Status of Women on the Policy Making Process: A California Case Study." Paper presented at the annual meeting of the American Political Science Association, Chicago, September 2-5, 1976.

Brown, David S. "The Public Advisory Board as an Instru-
    ment of Government." Public Administration Review 15
    (Summer 1955): 196-204.
Bryson, Lyman. "Notes on a Theory of Advice." Political
    Science Quarterly 66 (September 1951): 321-29.
Cartwright, Dorwin, and Zander, Alvin. "Individual Motives
    and Group Goals" Introduction." In Group Dynamics:
    Research and Theory. 2nd ed. New York: Harper and
    Row, 1953.
Clark, Peter B., and Wilson, James Q. "Incentive Systems:
    A Theory of Organizations." Administrative Quarterly
    (September 1961): 129-66.
Cobb, Roger W., and Elder, Charles D. Participation in
    American Politics: The Dynamics of Agenda Building.
    Baltimore Johns Hopkins Press, 1975.
Couture, James M. Public Advisory Bodies in the Executive
    Branch of the Federal Government. Master's thesis,
    American University, 1953.
Cronin, Thomas E., and Greenberg, Sanford D. The Presi-
    dential Advisory System. New York: Harper and Row,
    1969.
Cronin, Thomas E., and Thomas, Norman C. "Federal
    Advisory Processes: Advice and Discontent." Science
    (February 1971): 6-23.
Dean, Alan L. "Ad Hoc Commissions for Policy Formulation?"
    In The Presidential Advisory System, edited by Thomas
    E. Cronin and Sanford Greenberg. New York: Harper
    and Row, 1969.
Dean, John P., and Whyte, W. F. "How Do You Know If the
    Informant Is Telling the Truth?" Human Organization.
Deniston, O. L., Rosenstock, I. M., and Getting, V. A.
    "Evaluation of Program Effectiveness." Public Health
    Reports 83 (April, 1968): 323-34.
Derthick, Martha. "Commissionship - Presidential Variety."
    Public Policy (Fall 1971).
Dexter, Lewis A. Elite and Specialized Interviewing. Evans-
    ton, Ill.: Northwestern University Press, 1970.
Dill, William R. "Environment as an Influence on Managerial
    Autonomy." Administrative Science Quarterly 2 (March,
    1958): 409-43.
Dolbeare, Kenneth M. Political Change in the United States: A
    Framework for Analysis. New York: McGraw-Hill, 1974.
Drew, Elizabeth. "On Giving Oneself a Hotfoot: Government
    by Commission." Atlantic Monthly 221 (May 1968): 45-49.
Dye, Thomas R. Politics in States and Communities. 3rd Ed.,
    Englewood Cliffs, New Jersey: Prentice-Hall, 1977.
Dye, Thomas R., and Zeigler, L. Harmon. The Irony of
    Democracy. Belmont, Calif.: Dixbury Press, 1971.
Edleman, Murray. Politics as Symbolic Action: Mass Arousal
    and Quiescence. Chicago: Academy Press, 1971.

_____. The Symbolic Use of Politics.   Urbana: Uni-
versity of Illinois Press, 1967.

Elazer, Daniel. American Federalism: A View from the States.
2nd ed. New York: Thomas Y. Crowell Co., 1972.

Etzioni, Amitai. A Comparative Analysis of Complex Organizations. New York: Free Press, 1975.

_____. Modern Organizations. Englewood Cliffs, N. J.:
Prentice-Hall, 1964.

_____. "Two Approaches to Organizational Analysis: A
Critique and a Suggestion." Administrative Science
Quarterly 5 (September 1960): 257-78.

_____. "Why Task-Force Studies Go Wrong." Wall Street
Journal, July 9, 1968, p. 18.

Eulau, Heintz, and Prewitt, Kenneth. Labyrinths of Democracy. Indianapolis: Bobbs-Merrill, 1973.

Eulau, Heinz, Wahlke, John C., Buchanan, William and
Ferguson, Leroy C. "The Role of the Representative."
American Political Science Review, 52 (1959): 742-56.

Flexner, Eleanor. Century of Struggle: The Women's Rights
Movement in the United States. Cambridge, Mass.:
Harvard University Press, 1959.

Freeman, Jo. The Politics of Women's Liberation: A Case
Study of an Emerging Social Movement and Its Relation to
the Policy Process. New York: David McKay Co., 1975.

Fried, Robert C. "Comparative Urban Research." University
of California at Los Angeles, European Urban Research,
Working Paper No. 1. Reissued September 1973.

Galloway, George B. "Presidential Commissions." Editorial
Research Reports 1 (May 1931): 359-60.

Georgopoulos, B. S., and Mann, Floyd C. The Community
General Hospital. New York: MacMillan Co., 1962.

Georgopoulos, B. S., and Tannebaum, Arnold S. "A Study of
Organizational Effectiveness." American Sociological
Review 22 (October 1957): 534-40.

Gill, Norman N. "Permanent Advisory Commissions in the
Federal Government". Journal of Politics 2 (November
1940): 411-35.

Githens, Marianne, and Prestage, Jewel L. A Portrait of
Marginality. New York: David McKay Co., 1977.

Gordon, Raymond L. Interviewing: Strategy, Techniques,
and Tactics. Rev. ed. Homewood, Ill.: Dorsey Press,
1975.

Gross, Edward. "The Definition of Organization Goals."
British Journal of Sociology 22 (September 1969): 277-94.

Gross, Neal, Mason, Ward S., and McEachern, Alexander W.
Explorations in Role Analysis. New York: John Wiley
and Sons, 1958.

Hall, Richard H. Organizations: Structure and Process.
Englewood Cliffs, N. J.: Prentice-Hall, 1972.

Hanser, Charles J. Guide to Decision: The Royal Commission. Totowa, N. J.: Bedminister Press, 1965.

Harari, Elrud. "Japanese Politics of Advice in Comparative Prospective: A Framework for Analysis and a Case Study." Public Policy 22 (Fall 1974): 537-77.

Hawley, Amos. "Community Power Structure and Urban Renewal Success." American Journal of Sociology 68 (January 1963): 422-31.

Hofferbert, Richard I., and Sharkansky, Ira. State and Urban Politics. Boston: Little, Brown and Co., 1971.

Hole, Judith, and Levine, Ellen. Rebirth of Feminism. New York: Quadrangle Books, 1971.

Hutcheson, John D., Jr., and Shevin, Jann. Citizens Groups in Local Politics: A Bibliographic Review. Santa Barbara, Calif.: Cleo Books, 1976.

Inglehart, Ronald. "The Silent Revolution in Europe: Intergovernmental Change in Post-Industrial Societies." American Political Science Review 65 (December 1971): 991-1017.

Kammerer, Gladys M. "Advisory Committees in the Legislative Process." Journal of Politics 15 (May 1953): 171-96.

Katz, Daniel, and Kahn, Robert L. The Social Psychology of Organizations. New York: John Wiley and Sons, 1966.

Kelly, Rita Mae, and Boutilier, Mary. "The Self Fulfilling Prophesy and the Study of Political Women." In The Study of Women and Politics: A Symposium Exploring Methodological Issues, edited by Sarah Schramm forthcoming.

Kirkpatrick, Jean J. Political Women. New York: Basic Books, 1974.

Krichmar, Albert. The Women's Rights Movement in the United States 1848-1870: A Bibliography and Sourcebook. Metuchen, N. J.: Scarecrow Press, 1972.

Lewis, Eugene. American Politics in a Bureaucratic Age: Citizens Constituents, Clients, and Victims. Cambridge, Mass.: Winthrop Publishers, 1977.

Lincoln, Richard et. al. "The Court, the Congress, and the President: Turning Back the Clock on the Pregnant Poor." Family Planning Perspectives 9 (September/ October 1977): 210-11.

Lipsky, Michael. "Protest as a Political Resource." American Political Science Review 62 (December 1978).

Lockwood, Maren Carden. The New Feminist Movement. New York: Russell Sage Foundation, 1974.

Lowi, Theodore J. The Politics of Disorder. New York: Basic Books, 1971.

Lynn, Naomi. "Women in American Politics: An Overview." In Women: A Feminist Perspective, edited by Jo Freeman. Palo Alto, Calif.: Mayfield Publishing Co., 1975.

March, James G., and Simon, Herbert A. Organizations. New
    York: John Wiley, 1958.
March, Carl M. Presidential Commissions. New York: King's
    Crown Press, 1945.
Martin, Del, and Lyon, Phyllis. Lesbian/Women. San Fran-
    cisco: Glide Publications, 1972.
Mead, Margaret, and Kaplan, Frances Bagley, eds. American
    Woman: Report of the President's Commission on the
    Status of Women and Other Publications of the Commis-
    sion. New York: Charles Scribner's Sons, 1965.
Michels, Roberto. Political Parties. Translated by Eden Paul
    and Cedar Paul. New York: Dover, 1959.
Mitchell, Joyce M., and Mitchell, William C. Political Analysis
    and Public Policy. Chicago: Rand McNally and Co.,
    1969.
Mohr, Lawrence B. "The Concept of Organizational Goal."
    American Political Science Review 58 (June 1973).
Molnar, Joseph J., and Rogers, David L. "Organizational
    Effectiveness: An Empirical Comparison of the Goal and
    System Resource Approaches." The Sociological Quarterly
    17 (Summer 1976): 401-13.
Mott, Paul E. The Characteristics of Effective Organizations.
    New York: Harper and Row, 1972.
New York Times, August 1, 1965, p. 6.
Nicholson, Jeanne. "Perceptions of Organizational Goals and
    Effectiveness: A Study of Four Metropolitan Washington
    Women's Commissions." Ph.D. dissertation, Johns Hopkins
    University, 1976.
Olson, Mancur, Jr. The Logic of Collective Action: Public
    Goods and the Theory of Groups. New York: Schocken
    Books, 1971.
Perl, Martin. "The Science Advisory System: Some Obser-
    vations." Science 173 (1971): 1211-15.
Perrow, Charles. "The Analysis of Goals in Complex Or-
    ganizations." American Sociological Review 26 (December
    1961): 854-66.
Pinard, Maurice. "Structural Attachments and Political
    Support in Urban Politics: The Case of Fluoridation
    Referendums." American Journal of Sociology 67 (March
    1963): 513-26.
Pitkin, Hanna. The Concept of Representation. Berkeley:
    University of California Press, 1967.
Piven, Frances Fox, and Cloward, Richard A. Poor People's
    Movements: Why They Succeed and How They Fail. New
    York: Pantheon, 1978.
Popper, Frank. The President's Commissions. New York:
    Twentieth Century Fund, 1970.
Price, James L. Organizational Effectiveness: An Inventory
    of Propositions. Homewood, Ill.: Richard D. Irwin,
    1968.

_____. "The Study of Organizational Effectiveness." Sociological Quarterly 13 (Winter 1972): 3-15.

Primack, Joel, and Von Hippel, Frank. Advice and Dissent. New York: Basic Books, 1974.

Pross, A. Paul, ed. Pressure Group Behavior in Canadian Politics. Scarborough, Ontario: McGraw-Hill Ryerson, 1975.

Richardson, Stephen A., et. al. Interviewing: Its Forms and Functions. New York: Basic Books, 1965.

Rush, Jerrold G. "Political Participation in America: A Review Essay." American Political Science Review 70 (June 1976): 583-91.

Salzner, George T. "The Policy Process and the Uses of National Government Commissions." The Western Political Quarterly 30 (September 1971): 438-48.

Schattschneider, E. E. The Semisovereign People. New York: Holt, Rinehart, and Winston, 1960.

Sigel, Roberta S. "Citizen Committees - Advice vs. Consent." Transaction (May 1967): 47-52.

Simon, Herbert A. "On the Concept of Organizational Goal." Administrative Science Quarterly 9 (June 1964): 1-22.

Steggert, Frank X. Community Action Groups and City Government: Perspectives from Ten American Cities. Cambridge, Mass.: Ballinger Publishing Co., 1975.

Stewart, Debra. "Taxeconomic Development in Women's Policy Studies: A Proposed Direction." Department of Political Science, North Carolina State University, 1977.

Stogdill, Ralph M. Handbook of Leadership: A Survey of Theory and Research. New York: Free Press, 1974.

Sullivan, Linda E., and Kruzas, Anthony T. eds. Encyclo-pedia of Governmental Advisory Organizations. Detroit: Gale Research Co., 1973.

Sulzner, George T. "The Policy Processes and the Uses of National Governmental Study Commissions." Western Political Quarterly 24 (September 1971).

Thomas, Norman C., and Wolman, Harold L. "Policy Formu-lation in the Institutionalized Presidency: The Johnson Task Forces." In The Presidential Advisory System, edited by Thomas E. Cronin and Sanford D. Greenberg. New York: Harper and Row, 1969.

Thompson, James D. Organizations in Action: Social Science Bases of Administrative Theory. New York: McGraw-Hill Book Co., 1967.

Tolchin, Susan, and Tolchin, Martin. Clout: Women, Power and Politics. New York: Coward, McCann, and Geoghegan, 1973.

Urban Studies Group. Citizen Participation Group: A Report to the National Urban Observatory. Lawrence: Univer-sity of Kansas, 1970.

U.S. Department of Labor, Women's Bureau. Handbook for Commissions on the Status of Women. Madison: University Extension, University of Wisconsin in cooperation with the Women's Bureau, Employment Standards Administration, U. S. Department of Labor, 1968, 1974.

U.S. Department of Labor, Women's Bureau, Employment Standards Administration. "A Compilation of Data on State and Local Commissions on the Status of Women." Mimeographed. Washington, 1973, 1975.

U.S. President's Commission on the Status of Women. American Women. Washington, 1963.

"U.S. National Women's Agenda." Social Policy (March/April, 1976).

Verba, Sidney. "Democratic Participation." Annals of the American Academy of Political Science. Vol. 2: Social Goals and Indicators for American Society 373 (September 1967): 54.

Wahlke, John C. "Policy Demands and System Support: The Role of the Represented." British Journal of Political Science 1 (1971): 271-90.

Wahlke, John C., Eulau, Heinz, Buchanan, William, and Ferguson, Leroy. The Legislative System. New York: McGraw-Hill, 1962.

Warner, W. Keith. "Problems in Measuring the Goal Attainment of Voluntary Organizations." Journal of Adult Education 19 (Fall, 1956): 3-14.

Warriner, Charles K. "The Problem of Organizational Purpose." Sociological Quarterly 6 (Spring 1965): 139-46.

Wilensky, Harold L. Organizational Intelligence. New York: Basic Books, 1967.

Williams, John A. "Political Leadership and Governmental Performance." Comparative Studies Association, Comparative Interdisciplinary Section, Working Paper No. 65. April 1976.

Wilson, James Q. Political Organizations. New York: Basic Books, 1973.

Wolanin, Thomas R. Presidential Advisory Commissions: Truman to Nixon. Madison: University of Wisconsin Press, 1975.

Wright, Deil S. "The Advisory Commission on Intergovernmental Relations: Unique Features and Policy Orientation." Public Administration Review 25 (September, 1965): 193-202.

Yuchtman, Ephraim, and Seashore, Stanley E. "System Resource Approach to Organizational Effectiveness." American Sociological Review 32 (December, 1967): 891-903.

Zald, Mayer N. "Comparative Analysis and Measurement of Organizational Goals: The Case of Correctional Institutions for Delinquents." Sociological Quarterly 4 (Summer 1963): 206-30.

Ziegler, L. Harmon, and Peak, G. Wayne. Interest Groups in
    American Society. Englewood Cliffs, N. J.: Prentice-
    Hall, 1972.

Index

About the Author

DEBRA W. STEWART is an associate professor of political science at North Carolina State University. She has edited a book entitled <u>Women in Local Politics</u> and has published several scholarly works including articles in <u>Publius</u>, <u>Policy Studies Journal</u>, <u>Public Administration Review</u>, and <u>Women and Politics</u>.